1688–1988
TIME FOR A NEW CONSTI

Also by Richard Holme

PARTNERS IN ONE NATION (*editor with David Steel*)
THE PEOPLE'S KINGDOM

Also by Michael Elliott

THE ROLE OF LAW IN CENTRAL–LOCAL RELATIONS
HEARTBEAT LONDON: The Anatomy of a Supercity

1688–1988

Time for a New Constitution

Edited by

Richard Holme

and

Michael Elliott

MACMILLAN
PRESS

First published 1988

Published by
THE MACMILLAN PRESS LTD
Houndmills, Basingstoke, Hampshire RG21 2XS
and London
Companies and representatives
throughout the world

Typeset by Wessex Typesetters
(Division of The Eastern Press Ltd)
Frome, Somerset

Printed and bound in Great Britain at
The Camelot Press Ltd, Southampton

British Library Cataloguing in Publication Data
1688–1988: time for a new constitution.
1. Great Britain. Constitution. Reform
I. Holme, Richard, *1936–* II. Elliott,
Michael, *1947–*
344.102′3
ISBN 0–333–46701–9 (hardcover)
ISBN 0–333–46702–7 (paperback)

The Constitutional Reform Centre

Aims

The Constitutional Reform Centre, which was launched in the Autumn of 1984, provides a focus for those people in all parties and none who

> believe that the maintenance of rights and freedom for the citizen even within a parliamentary constitution cannot be guaranteed in the face of potential new threats;
>
> further believe that our constitution needs to be reformed to bring it into line with the needs of contemporary society and to remedy its weaknesses.

The Centre analyses and evaluates the structure, operation and interrelationship of British public institutions. It also acts to safeguard the concept of 'the Constitution' by encouraging understanding and discussion and making recommendations for reform where these are appropriate.

Contents

Preface

This book was conceived in a spirit of mischief. In 1987, it occurred to both of us that in the winter of 1988–1989 there were bound to be loads of celebrations of the Glorious Revolution and the Bill of Rights. We suspected that they would be self-congratulatory. A collective pat-on-the-back by the establishment. Yet neither of us thought that, 300 years after those momentous events, there was much to celebrate in the British constitution. We thought that those charged with thinking about the way in which Britain was governed had grown complacent; that there was an assumption that our arrangements were in all ways perfect, or – with a tweak here, a twist there – easily perfectible. This was not our view, and we knew enough people who shared our scepticism. So under the aegis of the Constitutional Reform Centre, we set about bullying a group of our friends to produce papers on their favourite subjects. Many of these papers were given at the annual Scarman seminars, run by the Centre, in the winter of 1987–88. This was invaluable, and our thanks go to all those who came along to the seminars and criticised the papers.

Our authors have been the very model of promptness; we know enough about editing collections of papers to understand that this is rare. Our editors at Macmillan have laboured mightily to bring out the book to a tight deadline. Truth to tell, we were ourselves the weak link in the chain. We would not have made it without support from Hilary Muggridge, the Director of the Constitutional Reform Centre and – most especially – from Fiona Watt, who did a lot more than keep us both on our toes. But did she ever do that. Our profound thanks to them both.

London RICHARD HOLME
MICHAEL ELLIOTT

Notes on the Contributors

Vernon Bogdanor is Fellow of Brasenose College, Oxford, and Member of Council of Hansard Society for Parliamentary Government. Publications include *Devolution* (1979), *The People and the Party System: The Referendum and Electoral Reform in British Politics* (1981), *Multi-Party Politics and the Constitution* (1983), *What is Proportional Representation? A Guide to the Issues* (1984), *Problems of Democratic Government* (1989). He has also edited a number of books including *The Blackwell Encyclopedia of Political Institutions* and *Constitutions in Democratic Politics* (1988). He was Special Adviser to the House of Lords Select Committee on the European Communities for its report on a Uniform Electoral Procedure for the European Parliament. He is also a frequent contributor to newspapers and journals. He is at present completing a book on comparative democratic government.

Michael Brock is Warden of St George's House, Windsor. He has just retired after ten years as Warden of Nuffield College, after spending nearly all of his career in Oxford University. He was a Fellow and Tutor of Corpus Christi College in Modern History and Politics from 1950 to 1966; Vice-President and Bursar of Wolfson College, 1967 to 1976; and one of Oxford's Pro-Vice-Chancellors, 1980–8. He is the author of *The Great Reform Act* (1973), and co-editor, with his wife, of *H. H. Asquith: Letters to Venetia Stanley* (1982). He holds an Honorary D.Litt. of Exeter University and Honorary Fellowships of his three Oxford colleges. He was awarded the CBE in 1981.

James Cornford is Director of the Nuffield Foundation and Chairman of the Council of the Campaign for Freedom of Information. From 1976 to 1980 he was Director of the Outer Circle Policy Unit and became involved in drafting legislation to replace the Official Secrets Act 1911 which has been introduced in Parliament in various forms by Sir Clement Freud, Mr Robin Cook MP, Mr Frank Hooley, the Rt Hon. David Steel MP and most recently by Mr Richard Shepherd MP.

Bernard Crick is Professor Emeritus of Politics at Birkbeck College,

University of London, and author of *The Reform of Parliament* (1964, 2nd edn 1968, rev. 2nd edn 1970), *In Defence of Politics* (1964, rev. edn 1982), *George Orwell: A Life* (1980), *Socialist Values and Time* (Fabian Tract 495), *Socialism* (1987) and, with David Blunkett, *Labour's Aims and Values: An Alternative Statement* (1988). He is working on a book about the relations of the nations of the British Isles.

Ralf Dahrendorf is Warden of St Antony's College, Oxford. Born in Hamburg, Germany, in 1929, he studied classics, philosophy and sociology in Hamburg and London. From 1958 to 1968 he was a Professor of Sociology in Tübingen and Konstanz. His political career led him into the Federal German Parliament and Willy Brandt's first government as a Minister of State in the Foreign Office. In 1970 he was appointed a Member of the Commission of the European Communities. From 1974 to 1984 he was Director of the London School of Economics. He is the author of numerous books, the most recent one being *The Modern Social Conflict: Essay on the Politics of Liberty*.

Nicholas Deakin has been Professor of Social Policy and Administration at Birmingham University since 1980. Previously, he worked first as a civil servant and then on a research programme in race relations funded by the Nuffield Foundation. After spending three years in the late 1960s researching and teaching at Sussex University, he went back to work in government, where he served as Head of the Central Policy Unit at the GLC. He has published books and articles on race relations, urban policy and new towns. His most recent publication is *The Politics of Welfare* (1987).

Michael Elliott is the industrial editor of *The Economist*. He has taught law at Northwestern University, the University of Warwick, and the LSE; was a member of the Central Policy Review Staff in the Cabinet office; and has been, successively, *The Economist*'s political and Washington correspondent. He is the author of *The Role of Law in Central–Local Relations* (1981) and more than forty papers on law and politics.

John Grigg is a journalist and historian. He was educated at Eton and New College, Oxford. He served with the Grenadier Guards, 1943–5, was Conservative Parliamentary candidate, Oldham West,

1950 and 1951, and is now a member of the SLD. He edited the *National and English Review*, 1954–60, was a columnist for the *Guardian*, 1960–70. He is now on the staff of *The Times* and writing vol. VI of the paper's history. He is author of *Two Anglican Essays*; *The Young Lloyd George*; *Lloyd George: The People's Champion* (Whitbread Prize); *Lloyd George: From Peace to War* (Wolfson Prize); *1943: The Victory that Never Was*; and *Nancy Astor: Portrait of a Pioneer*. He is a Fellow of the Royal Society of Literature, and is Chairman of the London Library.

Richard Holme, CBE, is the Chairman of the all-party Constitutional Reform Centre, Chairman of the all-party Rights Campaign and Adviser to the National Committee for Electoral Reform. He has written extensively on constitutional topics, his most recent book being *The People's Kingdom* (1987). He was co-editor with David Steel of *Partners in One Nation* (1985). He is a former President of the Liberal Party. He is an Associate Member of Nuffield College, Oxford.

William Plowden is Executive Director of the new UK Harkness Fellowships Program, New York. He was Director General of the Royal Institute of Public Administration, 1978–88, a civil servant (in the Central Policy Review Staff and the trade and industry departments), 1960–5, 1971–8, and a Lecturer in Government at the London School of Economics, 1965–71. He is the author of *The Motor Car and Politics in Britain* (1973), and (with Tessa Blackstone) of *Inside the Think Tank: Advising the Cabinet 1971–83* (1988).

The Rt Hon Lord Scarman, PC, OBE, Hon. MD, Hon. DCL. Educated at Radley, 1925–30, and Brasenose College, Oxford, 1930–4, where he gained First, Honour Moderations (Classics) and First Lit.Hum. Called to the Bar by Middle Temple 1936. 1940–5 RAF, administrative and special duties, OBE 1944. Practised at junior bar London 1946–57; QC 1957; High Court Judge (Probate, Divorce and Admiralty Division) 1961; Chairman, Law Commission 1965–72; Lord Justice of Appeal 1972–7; Lord of Appeal 1977–86; Chairman, Public Inquiry into Disorders in Northern Ireland 1969 (report 1972); Public Inquiry into Red Lion Square disorder, 1974; industrial court of inquiry into the Grunwick dispute 1978; Public Inquiry into Brixton disorders, 1981. Chairman Anglo-French Judicial Exchange 1986, 1987.

Introduction
Richard Holme

The tercentenary of the Glorious Revolution is an occasion not only for legitimate celebration but also for reflecting on the narrow limits of what was achieved.

Did Britain's constitutional settlement come too early? The Bill of Rights of 1688, which is shot through with the religious fears of another epoch difficult for us to comprehend, was primarily designed to protect Parliament against the King. It was an agreement between a native oligarchy and an imported monarch. It was neither, as the first constitutions of later democracies set out to be, a victory for popular sovereignty, an expression of the general will, nor was it an assertion of the liberties of the individual, a declaration of human rights.

The protection it offered was that which a contract offers, in this case a contract which set out a redefined relationship between those who henceforward were to share power in a prescribed way. It confirmed what the Civil War had decided, that the King could only reign with the consent of Parliament, and thus established a shared legitimacy. But the Bill of Rights did not concern itself with popular consent, nor did it purport to offer protection for the citizen against the State. As Lord Scarman says in his contribution to this volume: 'The weakness of the 1688 Settlement was its lack of democratic content.'

In the three hundred years which have followed, there have been two evolutionary changes which have modified the relationship between the high contracting parties to the settlement, without the revolutionary change which occurred later in other democracies and which might have stood the constitution on its head and imposed a different basis for power. The first has been the expansion of the franchise, through the series of nineteenth-century Reform Bills, women's suffrage in 1918 and 1928 and the lowering of the voting age in 1969. This has increased the authority of Parliament in relation to the monarch, and of the elected House of Commons in relation to the unelected Second Chamber. The second has been the steadily increasing apparatus of administration as society has grown more complex and the role of government more extensive so that state power is today exercised on a scale which would have been unimaginable to the grandees who placed William of Orange on the throne.

The sovereignty of the Crown in Parliament, as classically enunciated by A. V. Dicey in the nineteenth century, can be seen as an attempt to reconcile three phenomena: the continuing and historical legitimacy of the sovereignty of the Crown; the new and expanding claims to legitimacy of an elected Parliament; and the burgeoning reality of state power in the modern sense. What this reconciliation has provided in practice is the justification for unified and centralised power, with parliamentary over-representation for Scotland and Wales, while the Acts of Union swept Scotland and Ireland into Britain, making it one unitary parliamentary kingdom.

Constitutional debate has tended to concentrate historically on the rival claims to legitimacy of Crown and Parliament, the contracting parties of 1688, with the arguments settled on the whole in favour of Parliament, although the process has come near to breakdown on occasions as between 1910 and 1914 over Ulster. Meanwhile, behind the debate, the power of the state has continued to grow, carrying forward its Crown privileges and secrecy into the modern age but able to claim new legitimacy from a more broadly elected House of Commons. What has been missing from the debate for the most part, however, have been questions about how power should be exercised, its proper process and necessary limits.

The American Revolution posed a series of questions, which the US Constitution attempted to resolve, about the nature of political power: the need for checks and balances; the distribution of power between centre and locality; and the rights of citizens in relation to government and of minorities in relation to majorities. In Britain the blanket answer to such questions in modern times, has been to recite the simple mantra of 'parliamentary sovereignty' as if the presence of elected members was not only a necessary but a sufficient condition for the wise and just exercise of power. The 'rule of law' which Dicey envisaged as the twin pillar of the British constitution has fallen into neglect beside its more robust neighbour.

In the countries of continental Europe, the revolutions of the nineteenth century and the post-dictatorship settlements of Germany and Italy in the twentieth century produced constitutions which were designed to delimit and divide power within the state. We do not have their equivalent either in Britain.

Instead we have a theory of unlimited sovereignty, all the more dynamic because it is justified by a combination of two powerful ideas, the ancient majesty of the Crown and the vote of the people for an elected House of Commons, which have come together in our unwritten constitution.

Such limits as there are on the exercise of power, without institutional boundary, are provided by conventions. However, for conventions to be effective, there has to be an underlying political consensus which respects them and treats them as if they were rules. Yet in recent decades that consensus has begun to break down and with it the sanctity of the conventions. One example will suffice; the abolition of an elected tier of government, in the shape of the GLC and the Metropolitan Authorities, in 1985.

Partisanship sits well with unlimited sovereignty, so what we have achieved in effect in modern Britain is a system of party government, dedicated to its own purposes, and not only not obliged to share power within society but legitimised by a constitution with just one single overriding principle, that of parliamentary sovereignty. This system of party government is buttressed by the two themes – mandate and manifesto, originally the property of the Left but now used avidly by the Right as well to ensure that parliamentary sovereignty becomes party rule, or 'elective dictatorship'.

The principal justification which is traditionally offered for an unwritten constitution with conventions rather than a formal written constitution with rules is that of flexibility, and ease of adaptation to changing conditions. Yet, as the contributors to this book illustrate in various ways, rational reform is difficult to achieve both because there is no clear and shared set of values as to the nature and purpose of our constitutional arrangements which is shared throughout society and against which proposals for reform can be tested and also because any particular proposal for reform has only one way on to the statute book, which is through the support of a governing party with an implicit investment in the status quo. So we have a constitutional Catch-22, in which legitimate public interest in fair and rational government, over and above the interests of the government of the day, can only be articulated in terms of political opposition which may not survive the subsequent seductions of power. There is no reference point above, or even aside from the will of the government.

Michael Brock, in a fascinating historical grace-note about the haphazard origins of the Official Secrets Act, shows how in 1911 the Act had been directed against spies not towards muzzling the press but concludes that 'Section 2 of the Official Secrets Act has endured because ministers and opposition leaders hoping soon to be ministers, have shown a natural favour for it'.

Michael Elliott in his chapter speculates whether the emerging political agenda might include or even pivot around a new constitutionalism which in his words represents 'a healthier way in which the interests of governing and governed can be reconciled.' If so, what should find a place on that new agenda?

Lord Scarman calls for a Bill of Rights, based on the European Convention of Human Rights, which, with a new Parliament Act, might form temporary bulwarks until we had a written constitution 'based on the separation of powers; declaring the rights and liberties to be constitutionally protected; establishing a supreme constitutional court with jurisdiction to review executive and legislative action to ensure that it is within the limits set by the constitution; and requiring special procedures for the amendment of the constitution.'

Would the separation of powers concept apply not only to delimitation of the respective roles of Parliament, government and the judiciary but also to the way executive power is divided between the nation-state of the United Kingdom and the nations, regions and localities which comprise it?

Bernard Crick demolishes Blackstone's celebrated assertion that 'absolute power . . . must in all government reside somewhere' and makes a case for dispersed and shared power, for political rather than legal federalism for Scotland, Wales and the English regions.

He also reminds us of a Tocqueville's reproof to John Stuart Mill for linking liberty solely to the rights of individuals and his opinion, which Mill then adopted, that a plurality of intermediate institutions between the individual and the state was also a necessary sociological condition of liberty.

It is this pluralism which Nicholas Deakin perceives as being at risk from the centralist attack on the role of the periphery in recent years. He acknowledges that existing developments may have gone so far that a simple reversion to local government as a principal provider of local services is unlikely and argues instead for an explicitly pluralist solution in which elected local government changes its role from service provider to supervisor and contractor, working with the private and voluntary sectors, but still rooted firmly in the local community.

Looking through the other end of the constitutional telescope at Britain's centralised nation-state from the perspective of the European Community, Vernon Bogdanor also argues for the transfer of powers from the omnipotent nation-state, both downwards to the regions and localities of Britain and upwards to a European Community which he proposes should become more democratic and accountable. He concludes: 'The rationale for both policies is the same – that, in the modern world, the power of government is most effectively exercised when it is shared, rather than emanating only from one focal point.'

It is with the effective exercise of power that the other authors deal from varying perspectives, and in the process make the case for change and reform. James Cornford, picking up the question of official secrecy, introduced by Michael Brock, argues the case for a Freedom of Information Act and, disposing of the inevitable objections raised on grounds of cost and administration, identifies that the real objections are political. He quotes Lord Franks: 'Knowledge is power. It is important to recognise that the issue of open government is about power, political power, a shift in power, its redistribution.'

In any such shift the role of the civil service, the permanent government of officialdom, would be crucial. William Plowden refers to the 'delusion of British civil servants and ministers, understandable and dangerous, and shared with all others who wield governmental power, that one of the main tests of good government is that the will of the executive shall prevail.' He wonders: 'what are the effective limits to civil service obedience, loyalty and silence?' and expresses doubts about the idea that the traditional virtues of the civil service, a unifying tradition, a professional ethic and an accepted code of behaviour, can act as a constitutional constraint on arbitrary government, particularly when those very virtues are seen by some as increasingly inappropriate to a 'can-do' managerially-directed civil service.

That brings us back, as all British constitutional discussion does, to Parliament. But John Grigg sees Parliament too 'as more subservient.' He makes cogent criticisms of Parliament's internal working methods and the proliferation of placemen, pointing to a ministerial inflation from 57 in 1924 to over 100 on the payroll currently. He sees hope, however, in the select committees and recommends that their members should be elected by the House rather than appointed by the Whips.

He also suggests electoral reform, with which my own chapter deals, not so much from the traditional perspective of representation as from the effect of a choice-based system on party government, and on the nature of the parties themselves. I pose the possibility of a parliamentary and governmental system forced to come to terms with and organise itself around the poles of competition and cooperation.

Thus in different but often complementary ways the contributors to this volume have set out an agenda for constitutional reform analysing the inadequacy of our present arrangements and arguing for a more open, dispersed and rational way of allowing people to govern themselves effectively. This is so much the age of the economist that the traditional political virtues which make for a civil society are sometimes forgotten. Ralf Dahrendorf reminds us what the object of all our schemes and nostrums should be: 'The politics of liberty is about more life-chances for more people. Its condition and constitutional basis is civil society. A civil society is a society of citizens in the full sense of the word.' That is what the settlement of 1688 was not, and could not be, and what Britain is still waiting for.

I Retrospective

1 'Time and Chance': a Constitutional Retrospect

Michael Brock

'We Englishmen', Dickens's Mr Podsnap told the foreign gentlemen, 'are Very Proud of our Constitution . . . It Was Bestowed Upon Us by Providence.' The view which Dickens immortalised had been held for more than a century when he wrote *Our Mutual Friend.*[1] The figure of John Bull, epitomising English good sense and solidity, had appeared as early as 1712.[2] By that date the Revolution of 1688 and the Bill of Rights were seen as the turning point when England had taken the road to good order and progress.

We ought to honour the architects of the revolution settlement, rather than reviling them for failing to produce a wholly new constitution, duly entrenched. If British ideas on constitution-making have not progressed at all in three hundred years we shall indeed need to abandon any whiggish view of our history. The Bill of Rights of 1689 represented an attempt to deal more or less systematically with the salient constitutional problems of the time. Some of what are loosely called our 'constitutional laws' found their way on to the statute book more fortuitously than that. All constitutional arrangements reflect the balance of political forces in the era when they were passed. The Supreme Court of the United States 'follows the election returns', as Mr Dooley long ago observed.[3] All such arrangements enshrine, in one feature or another, the results of political accidents. This is particularly true of Britain, where constitution-making is part of the ordinary legislative process. Some of these accidents have had benign effects. The Habeas Corpus Amendment Act of 1679 would have been rejected, as it seems, by the House of Lords had Lord Norris, telling for the Noes, not been 'subject to vapours'. Burnet records:

> A very fat lord coming in, Lord Grey [telling for the Ayes] counted him for ten, as a jest at first: but seeing Lord Norris had not observed it, he went on with this misreckoning of ten: so it was reported to the House, and declared that they who were for the

Bill were the majority, though it indeed went on the other side: and by this means the Bill passed.[4]

Some of the accidents have proved less benign. Section 2 of the Official Secrets Act, 1911, has been in operation for more than seventy-five years. This Section was accepted by both Houses without discussion on the strength of an undertaking by the Liberal government that it would not be used to curb or punish disclosures in the press. 'The leading characteristic' of the main offence created by Section 2 is what the Franks Committee called in 1972 'its catch-all quality'. Under this section, for instance, a misdemeanour is committed by anyone receiving information if he has 'reasonable ground to believe that the person communicating it does so without authority', and 'is or has been employed under a person who holds or has held an office or contract' under the Crown. The recipient is not safe unless he can prove that the communication was 'contrary to his desire'.

The law on the publication of official secrets forms an area of great difficulty in any constitution. There are, however, some tests by which these laws may be judged. They ought to distinguish between disclosures of official information which may endanger the state and those which cannot do so, and between the duties of those who hold (or have held) official positions and those who do not. They ought to be as narrowly drawn as is compatible with the safety of the state and the effective conduct of its business, so that the criminal law is used only where other means of control are judged not to be effective. When confidential information has leaked, and a case is brought, the government's contention that the nation has been endangered or injured should not prevail without regard to circumstances. It should be possible for the accused to plead, as Mr Shepherd proposed recently, that official powers have been abused to the point at which disclosure is in the public interest.[5] In Section 2 of the Official Secrets Act, 1911, no account is taken of any of these criteria. It has been used in cases of disclosure in the press despite that long-forgotten governmental undertaking that it would not be so used. An account of its genesis may be of some interest.

British governments were troubled throughout the nineteenth century both by breaches of official trust and by the transmission of information to potentially hostile powers. In 1887 two incidents occurred, each of which combined both features. Some instructions to the Intelligence Department of the Navy were published in the press; and a dockyard draftsman sold confidential tracings and designs of warships, possibly to a foreign power. A measure which was first drafted as the Breach of Official Trust Bill was introduced in 1888 and enacted as the Official Secrets Act in 1889.[6] Its first section dealt with spying, its second with breaches of official trust; and this remained the pattern when the 1889 Act was widened and reinforced in 1911.

The press arrangements made during the Boer War aroused much criticism. In 1904 'control of the press during or in anticipation of war' was referred to the Committee of Imperial Defence, where it was decided that a 'Publication of Naval and Military Information Act' should be put into the statute book: it would be brought into effect by Order in Council whenever war might threaten.[7] On 21 June 1906 a 'meeting of representative journalists and newspaper proprietors' at the Royal United Service Institution gave the scheme a cautious blessing in principle; and the Prime Minister assured the Commons that the government intended to bring the matter forward 'early next year'.[8]

The Liberal government had inherited this plan from their Conservative predecessors. It was not popular with their most faithful supporters, to whom suggestions that war might be imminent were anathema. Why, asked Sir John Leng of the *Dundee Advertiser*, was wartime press control thought urgent?

> If there is any conceivable risk, is it not rather consequent on the reckless malevolence of a few unscrupulous journals which seize every occasion of writing in provocative and offensive terms of governments and peoples with whom all our interests as well as theirs are in favour of enduring peace?
>
> Believing as I do that the preservation of peace is the most patriotic of all policies, I cannot withhold my protest against an attempt to facilitate the letting slip of the dogs of war by muzzling the press.[9]

Objections such as these were widespread and strong enough to impose a delay which brought two important developments. On 30 July 1907 Viscount Esher asked in the Lords what were the safeguards against unauthorised publication of business letters passing among the highest in the land – the King and his predecessors, Viceroys of India, Ambassadors, and the members of cabinets. The Lord

Chancellor replied that the existing safeguards were far from adequate, since there would be very little chance of bringing copyright protection into play until the damage had been done.[10] Esher's plea for legislation could not be treated lightly. As a close friend of Edward VII, and one of the editors of Queen Victoria's letters, he knew as well as anyone what premature publication might entail. He was also a member of the Committee of Imperial Defence. On 2 December 1907, in a more startling development, the *Daily Express* published details of a naval gunnery trial, and outlined the defects in the Navy's armour-piercing shells and fire-control systems which this was supposed to have revealed.[11]

The government's tactics were now changed; and it was decided that the first step should be an amendment to the Official Secrets Act. Esher's diversion was not unwelcome. The less these problems were put into a wartime context, the more acceptable solving them might become to the Liberal backbenchers. Moreover, as the challenge from the German navy grew more serious, it was realised that disclosures in peacetime about naval design could be as dangerous as any leakage in war. The Amending Bill was introduced by the Lord Chancellor in the Lords on 16 March 1908. As breaches of official trust were not the target, Section 2 remained untouched. The new sections were aimed explicitly at those who might envisage *publishing* official secrets.[12]

The press could not be diverted from their fears of being muzzled in war. The Lord Chancellor's Bill never reached second reading.[13] A few months before it was introduced, the Newspaper Proprietors' Association delivered a devastating attack on its twin, the Publication of Naval and Military Information Bill.[14] This had been altered in an effort to assuage the worries of the Institute of Journalists.[15] The alterations included the creation of an Advisory Council to monitor wartime censorship. The proprietors claimed the whip hand: they objected to sharing membership of the Council with the news agencies and the Institute of Journalists. Giving priority to the Bill which would be operative in peacetime merely made the Government look dictatorial. A Liberal administration, write the military correspondent of *The Times*, has produced 'a most illiberal and retrograde measure'.[16] 'Armed with this measure,' the Liberal *Daily News* pronounced, 'any minister could safely suppress any scandal.'[17]

These attacks on the Lord Chancellor's Bill did not establish that nothing needed to be done. It had not been published a week before the naval and military authorities were appalled by a new defence revelation in the press. Enraged by Haldane's success at the War Office, and yet convinced that all Liberals were irresponsible pacifists at heart, the editor of the *Morning Post* sanctioned a reckless attack on a particularly sensitive aspect of the government's defence policy. On 21 March 1908 the *Morning Post* revealed the whole armament of Dover, gun by gun, except for the quick-firers on the breakwater, together with the exact strength of the garrison. This article, Naval Intelligence reported, 'must have been written by a soldier, and one who has had access to a good deal of official information.'[18] The incident highlighted the extent to which Conservative partisanship constituted a threat to national security: a good many officers in both navy and army were willing to bring pressure on the Government to increase defence expenditure by letting Conservative newspapers have defence secrets.[19]

Between October 1908 and March 1909 fears of German aggression increased sharply among the public, and indeed within the cabinet. It became public knowledge that the German yards were in a position to build and arm Dreadnought battleships on a scale, and at a speed, which exceeded the building programme announced.[20] On 5 November 1908 the Prime Minister spoke to his opposite number in the Commons about the international situation. In Balfour's words,

> Asquith . . . said, that, incredible as it might seem, the government could form no theory of the German policy which fitted all the known facts except that they wanted war . . . : the internal conditions of Germany were so unsatisfactory that they might be driven to the wildest adventures in order to divert national sentiment into a new channel.[21]

In March 1909 the Prime Minister appointed a sub-committee of the CID to review the security of defence information. This was more than a response to the popular alarms about German spies, though these had by now reached new heights. Beneath the absurdities of 'spy mania' lay an uncomfortable fact: the Government had evidence that the German system of espionage in Britain was comprehensive and efficient.[22] It seemed more than a coincidence that the head waiter of the Burlington Hotel, Dover, had been identified as a German artillery captain.[23]

While the sub-committee was at work the *Daily Mail* secured a defence scoop by publishing 'secret' particulars about the new British battleships. The sub-committee report included the views of the First Lord of the Admiralty on this case:

> In the present state of the law we are unable to prosecute the editor of this paper . . . ; and, even if we were to find out the person who gave the information . . . it would be undesirable to institute proceedings against him, since in doing so we should be compelled to vouch for the truth of the information published. Mr McKenna therefore considered it desirable that The Official Secrets Act, 1889, should be amended in such a manner as to enable the Government to prosecute persons who knowingly publish secret information.[24]

The sub-committee agreed that legislation was necessary, but, in the light of what had happened to the 1908 Bill, they recommended that the Amendment of the 1889 Act 'should only apply to actual espionage, and should not contain clauses, the tendency of which would be to restrict the freedom of the press.'[25] Two Bills were therefore recommended. The first, which was to strengthen the anti-espionage section (Section 1) of the Official Secrets Act, 1889, would be introduced by the Secretary of State for War. The second should 'have for its object the prevention of the publication of certain documents or information'. This should be introduced 'after negotiations with the representatives of the press have resulted in an agreement as to its provisions'.

Much of the confusion which followed resulted from the fact that the departments chiefly concerned with leakage to the press had divergent aims. The prime concern of the Admiralty was to keep secret during peacetime information about fleet dispositions and warship and weapon construction. The CID and the War Office were chiefly worried about security of information during a war crisis or a war. Other departments, led by the Treasury and the Home Office, were concerned with breaches of official trust over a wide range of subjects unconnected with defence. In 1909 information about undelivered old-age pension books appeared in the press before it had been given to Parliament. In the following year premature publication of the Report of the Welsh Church Commission was equally embarrassing.[26]

On 1 March 1910 Asquith appointed a new standing sub-committee of the CID to recommend on the whole question of wartime censorship. Negotiations with the press were then resumed, but proved as fruitless as ever.[27] The attitude of the editors and their staffs is understandable. While they knew that the press would be curbed in a war, they objected to being restricted whenever the

Government might declare a war emergency. It struck them as no less unfair that they should be punished while the officials who had given them the information would go free; yet they knew that this would be the result of any tightening in the legislation, partly because they would have to protect their sources, partly because the source, unlike the newspaper, could not be prosecuted without the admission that the information provided had been authentic. Penalties for the loss or theft of secrets, under which the receiver of the stolen goods would be punished while the thieving or careless watchman went free, did not accord with accepted views of fair play; and some of the 'watchmen' concerned held far higher positions than any to which a working journalist aspired. The 1909 battleship disclosures in the *Daily Mail* may show that such hesitations were not groundless; for the leak was traced to the First Sea Lord. Fisher had been talking in the Senior United Services Club to a deaf Admiral in the hearing of a waiter who, after service with the Fleet, had a friend in Fleet Street.[28]

Meanwhile Parliamentary Counsel produced the new version of the Official Secrets Act. No mention was made in this of the publication of prohibited material. The object was to widen the Act's scope so that it comprehended at all points, not merely officials and government contractors, but anyone who misused official secrets. Unless authorisation had been given, it would be an offence to acquire secret material under Section 1, or to receive, retain, or communicate it under Section 2. It seemed clear that, widened in this way, Section 2 could be used against the large-scale communicators, namely, the press men. On 4 November 1910 the Secretary of the Admiralty recorded Parliamentary's Counsel's view on this:

> As regards the newspapers, it might be held that for the press to communicate to the public certain information prejudicial to the interests of the State would be an offence under the Act; but Sir A. Thring considered that it would be better not to treat the Act as covering publication in the newspapers, unless the circumstances were very special. It was understood that the Home Secretary had a Bill drafted for his consideration.[29]

The Secretary of the Admiralty also noted that when the scope of the Act was widened, the opportunity had not been taken to differentiate between those convicted of breaking official trust and other offenders. He was assured by Parliamentary Counsel that this point had been discussed.[30]

Before the Official Secrets Bill could be introduced the Agadir crisis had begun to change the scene. The German gunboat *Panther* anchored off the Moroccan port of Agadir on 1 July 1911. For three months thereafter it seemed as if the resulting crisis might end in war. In September Britain's precautions against acts of war sabotage included the patrolling of the South Eastern Railway. The Bill came up for discussion in the Lords on 25 July as a war crisis measure. The Government's timing could not have been bettered. On the evening of 21 July Lloyd George had warned the Germans in his Mansion House speech that Britain would treat Morocco as an area 'where her interests were vitally affected': she was even prepared to go to war to enforce her rights there. It became clear during the next few days that this warning had caused intense anger in Germany and that the most acute phase of the crisis had been reached.[31] This was not their Lordships' only preoccupation on 25 July. Their amendments to the Parliament Bill had been down for discussion in the Commons on the previous day; and in an unprecedented scene the Prime Minister had been shouted down when trying to outline how the Government meant to deal with them.[32] In these conditions the Lords accepted the Official Secrets Bill without a division after a discussion which occupies only six columns of Hansard.[33]

There remained the problem of ensuring the Bill's swift passage through the Commons. The whips' office gave their opposite numbers the Government's undertaking that the Act when passed 'would be directed against the class of spies, and not for the purpose of muzzling the press'.[34] The assurance was accepted; and on 17 August the Chief Whip announced that the House would be asked to pass the Bill through all its stages on the following day. Austen Chamberlain responded for the opposition: 'We, of course, shall give our support in every way we can.'[35] It had long been the Opposition's tactic to support what they saw as the Government's fitful patriotism in the hope of increasing the protests from pacific Liberal backbenchers.

By Friday 18 August the railway strike was spreading rapidly: 200,000 railwaymen were said to be idle on that day. Writing many years later Hankey recalled the passage of the Bill through the House on that Friday afternoon as 'a masterly example of Parliamentary strategy'.[36] There was some protesting at the extreme haste; and a few legal points were raised, none of them bearing on Section 2; but only ten Members, all of them Liberal or Labour, voted against the Government in the one division called. The Government speakers did not repeat in the House the private undertakings which had been given about the press: there was no call for them to do so.[37] The *Morning Post* welcomed the protection against spying which the new Act, gave, although an article which had appeared in it, only two days earlier, on 'The Guardianship of British Forts', could have led, but for the Government's pledge, to prosecution under the new Section 2.[38]

The passage of the new Official Secrets Act into law gave the Government no ground for complacency. They still had to tackle the problem of controlling press statements and the Agadir crisis had thrown a harsh light on this. The CID reported early in 1913:

> Although the crisis of 1911 never reached the stage when it was considered wise formally to declare the existence of the precautionary period, certain steps were nevertheless taken by the Government; and notices appeared in the newspapers purporting to give correct information concerning the naval movements, the movement of coal, measures of precaution on board ships of war, the steps taken for strengthening the guards on magazines, and many other matters of importance from a naval and military point of view. It is clear that such revelations might well have afforded valuable information to an enemy; and a certain risk of prejudicing the issue of diplomatic negotiations towards a peaceful settlement was in fact involved.[39]

Precautionary moves lost half their value if they did not remain secret. Moreover as soon as they were revealed they might well be called provocative by a large part of the German press and by some members of the British Liberal Party.[40] To break the deadlock Haldane instructed the Assistant Secretary in the War Office, Reginald Brade, 'to enter into informal negotiations with the dominant press interests with the view of arriving at some friendly arrangement'.[41] The idea of such an arrangement was not new. In December 1907 the Director of Naval Intelligence had suggested asking for the cooperation of the press 'in preventing the publication of information likely to be of value to foreign countries'.[42] It was the air of urgency given to the problem by the Agadir crisis which made an 'arrangement' an attractive alternative to new legislation.

Brade held his discussions with the proprietors of the main London papers, who proved much more amenable than the journalists had been. He quickly succeeded in securing the arrangements which eventually became the D Notice system. Early in 1913 the CID subcommittee put their Publication of Naval and Military Information

Bill into cold storage. 'It would be useless', they reported, 'to attempt legislation in advance of the outbreak of war. An effective Act would not be secured, and the present agreement with the press would almost certainly be lost.'[43]

By the end of 1911, proprietors such as Northcliffe and Riddell had much to gain from an agreement. They valued their links with the Government and injudicious defence scoops were too obviously unpatriotic to be profitable. Most proprietors had little liking for the theme of defence. Those who controlled the Liberal press still regarded Germany's aggressive designs as a Tory fiction; they wanted to play down external threats as far as they could.[44] The position of the other press magnates was more complex. The discussion of defence was apt to raise the conscription issue, which every Conservative politician regarded as a specific for losing votes. Moreover it was difficult to write about the Navy without taking sides in the Fisher–Beresford quarrel. Finally, the question of the British Expeditionary Force divided Northcliffe from most of his staff. On 4 August 1914 he still believed that no British soldier should leave Britain's shores.[45] Irish Home Rule was a far better ground than defence from which to launch press attacks on the Government.

None the less Brade explored the degree to which he could claim statutory backing for his arrangements. In November 1912 he told the CID sub-committee that on one occasion in that year the Director of Public Prosecutions had seen an editor 'and warned him that the Official Secrets Act might be used against him.'[46] Further action of that kind was ruled out of court at a sub-committee meeting on 26 November 1912, when Seely, by now Secretary of State for War, was in the chair. Seely explained that he had asked the Attorney-General whether the Official Secrets Act, 1911, could be used 'against a newspaper'. The reply had been 'that the Government were bound in honour not to employ the Act against editors or other persons connected with the press.' Seely then referred, in words which have been quoted above, to the grounds on which the House of Commons had been induced to pass the Bill as an emergency measure. Brade asked whether succeeding governments would be similarly bound. The Assistant Treasury Solicitor thought this an idle query, since an editor would be in little danger of conviction 'if a jury had any suspicions as to the intentions of the Act.'[47]

With the war that world disappeared. In 1916 the deputy chairman of the publishers of the *Military Mail* was sentenced under Section 2 to two months' imprisonment along with the War Office clerk who had passed him information. In that some of this information was critical of senior War Office officials its publication might conceivably have been held to prejudice national safety. In 1926, however, a conviction under Section 2 was secured in a press case where neither national security, nor indeed any obvious national interest, were involved at all. A series of newspaper articles written by a retired governor of Pentonville Prison revealed remarks made to him by a convicted murderer just before execution. The defence that action under Section 2 had to be limited to cases where the national interest was involved was advanced and failed: and the ex-governor was fined.[48]

The view that the 1911 Official Secrets Act was concerned solely with spying died hard, however. It was reinforced by a statement from the Attorney-General (Sir Gordon Hewart) during the passage of the 1920 Official Secrets Act through the Commons.[49] Some of those who gave evidence to the Franks Committee in 1971–2 argued that Section 2 'was not intended by the Government of the day or by Parliament to have the catch-all quality' later attributed to it. The Committee rejected this contention: they were sure 'that the Bill had, and was intended by the Government to have, wider scope.'[50] The account given above may cast some doubt on the Committee's view about this. Several of our constitutional arrangements had mysterious origins. None of them started more strangely than Section 2 of the Official Secrets Act.

Section 2 has endured because ministers, and opposition leaders hoping soon to be ministers, have shown a natural favour for it. The same applies a little less obviously to other constitutional arrangements. A first-past-the-post electoral system of single-member constituencies depresses the chances of any group in the centre. It thus runs counter to the strongest social currents of our time. These were succinctly delineated by Professor Ralf Dahrendorf in a recent lecture:

> At the end of the line . . . there is . . . the emergence of a very large category of democratic citizens, people who would probably describe themselves as middle-class, and who benefit from a system for which even the mild term, democratic class struggle, is too fierce. These two-thirds, possibly three-quarters of all citizens of modern free societies, have a common interest in the maintenance

> of political institutions which guarantee economic growth and social peace; their divergent interests are comparatively minor; moreover, such differences do not lend themselves to the formation of classes and class-based parties. Indeed . . . this majority . . . is one class with all the internal distinctions and differences which have always been characteristic of classes. If one likes paradox, one might call it the citizens' class; . . . this is, of course, also the 'one nation' class, the class of 'consensus politics'. . . . At times one might be forgiven for simply calling it *the* class; it is in any case the majority class.[51]

Exactly how far these words apply to present-day Britain is a controversial question; but it would be widely accepted that the main social tendency nowadays is as Professor Dahrendorf describes it. Two factors explain the survival in Britain of an electoral system which is strikingly at odds with this new world. In the first place, majorities in both the Conservative and Labour parties have thought a change to run counter to their interests. Secondly, any change to give more adequate representation to the centre is seen as a move towards weak and unstable governments.

It can be argued that neither view is particularly well-based. A glance at our electoral history shows political parties to be as fallible in judging their electoral interests as in other matters. The attitude of Labour and Liberal leaders early in this century towards proportional representation may be cited to illustrate an interesting mixture of vision and blindness. In the prewar period Ramsay MacDonald would not accept Snowden's advocacy of proportional representation. 'We shall supplant the Liberals', he would say; 'and then the system which now seems so unfair will work in *our* favour.'[52] During the war the Liberal leaders showed none of MacDonald's farsightedness on the issue. In January 1917 the Speaker's Conference reported unanimously in favour of proportional representation in a limited number of seats. Neither Lloyd George nor Asquith gave the recommendation solid or consistent support. Both seem to have been swayed by local considerations. To Lloyd George proportional representation represented a threat to the Liberal dominance of Welsh constituencies. Asquith did not want the seat he had held since 1886 merged into a multi-Member constituency comprising the whole County of Fife.[53] The Liberals were to pay heavily for these mistakes. Less than a year later Asquith suffered a humiliating defeat in East Fife from which proportional representation would have saved him. Lloyd George lived to see the Liberals lose their greatness even in Wales.

The fact that some political leaders may hold short or self-regarding views constitutes only one ingredient in the fallibility of predictions about constitutional change. In this area all prophecies, especially perhaps those of doom, should be received with reserve. The Great Reform Bill was piloted through the Commons by Lord Althorp who nearly always showed sound practical judgement. Yet he told a colleague early in 1833 of his hope that in the reformed House of Commons governments would be able to dispense with whips.[54] Althorp's mistaken hopes were matched by the equally mistaken forebodings of his great antagonist, Sir Robert Peel. In July 1832, a few weeks after the Reform Bill had reached the statute book, Peel warned the Commons of his expectation 'that apprehensions would prevail for the security of property – apprehensions which were likely to affect considerably . . . the productive powers of the country – and that the political excitement would continue as rife, and the political unions as flourishing and as noisy, as ever.'[55] It can be assumed that, while many of the hopes about constitutional reform must be dupes, some of the fears will turn out to have been liars.

Notes

Quotations from Crown Copyright records are reproduced by kind permission of the Controller, Her Majesty's Stationery Office.

1. This was first published in monthly numbers in 1864–5.
2. In a pamphlet by John Arbuthnot (1667–1735).
3. 'Mr Dooley', the fictional creation of Finley Peter Dunne, first appeared in a Chicago newspaper in the 1890s and gained national recognition in the 1896 Presidential campaign. His sage comments were recorded in a thick Irish brogue.
4. *History of His Own Time*, I.485 (Folio Edition). According to Onslow's note the story is borne out by a comparison between the number of peers recorded as present in the Minute Book and the numbers in the division.
5. Protection of Official Information Bill, Clause 7: see Mr Shepherd's second reading speech, 15 January 1988: *Parl.Deb.*, Commons, 6 Ser., 125.566.
6. *Home Office, Departmental Committee on Section 2 of the Official Secrets Act, 1911* (Franks Committee), Cmnd 5104: vol. 1 (Report), App. iii, 121–2.
7. CID, 63rd Meeting. See CID Papers 39B and 82B: PRO.
8. *The Times*, 22 June, 8b,c; 27 June 1906: *Parl.Deb.*, 4 Ser., 159.954.

9. Open letter to A. R. Byles, 19 June 1906.
10. *Parl.Deb.*, 4 Ser., 179.716–721.
11. 2 December. *HMS Hero*, an obsolete warship had been bombarded and sunk as a test of naval firepower.
12. *Parl.Deb.* 186.104. For preparation of the Bill see memo. by Director of Naval Intelligence, 9 December 1907 (minuted), and Secy., Admiralty to Secy., War Office, 30 January 1908: PRO ADM 116/1058; F. F. Liddell (Parl.Counsel) to Secy., Admiralty, 23 January 1908, and Secy., Admiralty to Lord Chancellor's office (official letter and coverer), 22 February 1908: ADM 1/8030.
13. *Parl.Deb.*, 190.1474–80; *Journals and Letters of Visc. Esher*, ii (1934). 257–8. The Bill is in HL, Bills 1908, Vol. 4.
14. Manifesto, 6 February 1908: PRO ADM 116/1058.
15. As expressed at the Institute's 20th annual conference: *The Times*, 19 September 1907, 6b.
16. 7 May 1908.
17. 16 May 1908. For the reaction to the government's change of tactics of a retired naval officer particularly interested in security and defence problems see *Parl.Deb.*, 190.1477 (Ellenborough).
18. PRO, ADM.1/8030, f. 23; 21 March.
19. The invasion question, by stimulating controversy between the Blue Water and Bolt-from-the-Blue schools, provided a temptation to each side to bolster its case with selective revelations. The press reports about the 1909 naval manoeuvres contravened Admiralty orders: 13 July 1909, Lords Commissioners to Fleet Commanders: ADM 116/1058.
20. See, for instance, *The Times*, 15 October 1908, 5f; 30 November 1908, 8c.
21. K. Young, *Balfour* (1963) G. Bell & Sons, London, p. 271, quoting Balfour to Lansdowne, 6 November.
22. Grey's minute on Dumas's report of 3 February 1908: *Brit. Docs. War*, vi (1930), 117; *Quarterly Review*, 209 (July 1908), 295–6. See also G. Steinhauer and B. T. Felstead, *The Kaiser's Master Spy* (1930), John Lane, The Bodley Head, London, pp. 48–50. Steinhauer 'had forty agents in England' according to his statement after the war. He stressed that the agents were not fully trained spies and that their pay had been meagre. For the watch on these agents from 1911 see W. S. Churchill, *The World Crisis*, Thorton Butterworth, London, i (1923).52,211.
23. A. J. A. Morris, *The Scaremongers* (1984), Routledge & Kegan Paul, London, p. 156. This is based on Edmonds's unpublished memoirs. The statement in CAB 16/8, p. 16 is milder: 'Headwaiter suspected of being an officer. Admitted he was an NCO in a fortress artillery regiment.'
24. CID Paper 47-A: Report, 24 July 1909, Section 11: PRO CAB 16/8. Haldane was chairman of this sub-committee. Under cover of commenting on the new edition of F. J. Jane's *Fighting Ships*, the *Daily Mail* (23 June 1909,8b) had revealed that the British super-Dreadnought, planned but not then laid down, would fire ten 13.5-inch guns on either broadside.

25. Ibid., Section 12.
26. Franks Report (Cmnd. 5104), App. iii, 11, p. 122. *Parl. Deb.*, Commons, 1909 ix. 391–2, xi.9; 5 Ser.xx.277. The Welsh Church Commissioners were known to be at odds with each other on party lines. When the Director of Public Prosecutions and the Treasury Solicitor suggested amendment of the Official Secrets Act as the cure for such leaks, the Home Office considered: 'it is hardly worth legislating to deal merely with the case of leakage of reports of Royal Commissions' (PRO, HO45/11844; minute, 2 January 1911). The substance of the Welsh Church Report had appeared in the press long before 31 October 1910 when the *Daily Mail* and *South Wales Daily News* published their summaries of the final version (for a reference to this see *Manchester Guardian*, 11 November 1910).
27. 28 October 1910, Sydney Brooks's report: CAB 17/91, B-23 (28).
28. The author's father, then a young Admiralty official, had the duty of investigating how this leak had occurred. Fisher had uttered his usual dire threats against the culprit. For Fisher's relations with the press see A. J. Marder, *From the Dreadnought to Scapa Flow*, Oxford University Press, Oxford, i (1961). 82. For leaks by political leaders see R. Jenkins, *Asquith* (rev. edn., 1978), Collins, London, pp. 303–5; eds. M. and E. Brock, *H. H. Asquith: Letters to Venetia Stanley*, Oxford University Press, Oxford (1982), p. 107.
29. PRO ADM 1/8030. Graham Greene's handwriting is not quite clear in this minute.
30. Graham Greene to Arthur Thring and reply, 24 January and 1 February 1911: ADM 1/8030, ff. 60, 65.
31. See *The Times*, 25 July, 5b.
32. *Parl. Deb.*, Commons, 5 Ser., 28.1467–1473.
33. *Parl. Deb.*, Lords, 5 Ser., 9.641–7.
34. CID Paper 167–B, 31 January 1913, p. 11: PRO CAB 4/5.
35. *Parl. Deb.*, Commons, 5 Ser., 29.2122.
36. *Supreme Command* (1961), (i)115.
37. *Parl. Deb.*, 29.2251–58.
38. 2 September, 7b; 4 September, 7b. Although the facts stated in the article were common knowledge in the localities concerned it caused great anger in the CID: CAB 17/91, B-23(38). It could have been brought within Section 2(1) of the Act, since it contained 'information which related to prohibited places'.
39. CID Paper 167-B, section 5.
40. See, for instance, the *Nation*, 1 August 1914 (p. 657) on 'certain needless, dangerous, and ill-advised naval precautions'.
41. CID Paper 167-B, section 13.
42. 9 December: ADM 116/1058.
43. CID Paper 167-B, section 23. Esher had favoured an approach to the proprietors in July 1909: CID Paper 47-A, p. 11.
44. See, for the *Daily Chronicle*, P. Gibbs, *Adventures in Journalism*, Heinemann, London (1923), pp. 204–10; R. C. K. Ensor, *England, 1870–1914*, Oxford University Press, Oxford (1936), p. 484, n. 1. The

Westminster Gazette was the most realistic of the Liberal papers where German ambitions were concerned.

45. Tom Clarke, *My Northcliffe Diary*, Victor Gollancz, London (1931), pp. 65–7. For Northcliffe's views on press security in war see his letter to Churchill, 1 December 1911: *Churchill, Companion Volumes, 1901–1914*, Heinemann, London (1969), ed. Randolph S. Churchill, pp. 1348–9.
46. 5 November, memo. by Brade: CID Paper 167-B, p. 24.
47. CID Paper 167-B, p. 11.
48. Franks Report (Cmnd 5104), App. ii, p. 116.
49. 16 December 1920: *Parl.Deb.*, 136.966.
50. Report, section 53.
51. *Law and Order*, Hamlyn Trust, Boulder, Colorado, 1985, p. 23.
52. This account of MacDonald's contention was given to the author by the late Sir Robert Ensor, who had known MacDonald well in the pre-war years. Although Ensor was a most accurate reporter, these should not be given quite the status of verbatim remarks.
53. 30 January 1918: *Parl.Deb.*, 101.1636–7. Asquith was opposing the PR scheme as it had emerged, greatly enlarged, from the Lords. See Martin Pugh, *Electoral Reform in War and Peace, 1906–1918*, Routledge & Kegan Paul, London (1978), p. 164.
54. Letter to Sir James Graham undated, Graham Mss.: M. Brock, *Great Reform Act* (1973), p. 167. Mr Vernon Bogdanor has recently drawn attention to an even more striking instance of 'romanticism' in electoral reform. In 1884 both Gladstone and Salisbury expected single-member constituencies with fairly drawn boundaries to produce, in Gladstone's phrase, 'the representation of minorities . . . a very large diversity of representation': *Parl.Deb*, 3 Ser., 294.380.
55. 27 July: *Parl.Deb.*, 3 Ser., 14.875.

2 Constitutionalism, Sovereignty and Politics

Michael Elliott

I

In the last quarter of a century, some of Britain's most distinguished political and legal scholars have asserted that modern British government can be fruitfully examined from a 'constitutional' perspective. This has not been a simple descriptive exercise; more or less openly, those who have been dedicated to this enterprise have also believed that attention to the constitutional aspect of British government can help identify some worthwhile reforms. Cornford has neatly put the thesis in the form of a negative:[1] 'there has been a failure to think constructively about the nature of public authority, the state and the use of the courts as a constitutional resource . . . having in an early constitutional revolution got certain fundamentals settled, we have not gone on to think through or to deal with the consequences of the enormous growth of governmental activity'.

The critical axiom of those who have argued for a constitutional perspective, it seems to me, is that the exercise of certain forms of power needs a particular and special justification. At the most trivial, the power that I have to sit at a wordprocessor and write a chapter for a book does not raise a constitutional question; nor does the power I have to contract with a painter for the redecoration of my living room; nor does the decision of *The Economist* to shift part of its printing from one plant to another. Not all decisions that I, my painter or *The Economist* take are purely private ones – ones of interest only to us – but there is nothing about any of us which would make constitutional scholars spend more than a millisecond worrying about us. For a range of other people and institutions who exercise power, however, this is not the case. For these 'constitutional actors' – including parliament, the courts, ministers and civil servants – the constitutional perspective asserts that power can only be exercised in certain specific ways, according to certain forms. More than that, constitutionalism also claims, if only implicitly, that some exercises of those powers (for example, those which impinge on the rights of the individual) must be justified by reference to certain timeless principles, not simply by the exigency of the moment. Constitutionalism, in other words, requires that certain people and institutions should, at certain times, behave in particular ways – it posits a specialness about the actions with which it is concerned.

If they are honest, those who have argued for such a perspective on modern Britain are duty-bound to admit that their work has been an almost total failure. Consider, as examples, two areas to which constitutionalists have devoted an inordinate amount of time over the last 25 years. First, civil liberties. This, hardly a subject worthy of study in law schools or political science departments in the 1950s, is now a matter on which courses and books by the score are prepared. Yet the British approach to civil liberties has changed not a jot. If a government wants to restrict the liberty of its subjects, it may do so by seeking parliamentary approval for legislation in a manner identical to the approval it would seek for a power to build a new lighthouse. Once passed, decisions taken under the civil liberty-restraining legislation are different in legal kind not a whit from those taken in any other, mundane, concern of government. They are subject to no special procedures, susceptible to no specific review.

Secondly, consider the proposition – again, one which has been much in the minds of commentators – that the territorial division of public power raises certain fundamental questions.[2] Here, for those committed to the constitutional perspective, recent history has been particularly gloomy. Not only did the 1970s question of devolution proceed as if constitutional matters had nothing to do with the case;[3] more recently, a government has been able to emasculate the executive powers and financial autonomy of local authorities without admitting any suggestion that its actions needed to be carefully – and specially – justified.

The point here is not to argue that recent governments have trampled on civil liberties, or to assert that local governments pre-1979 were the apotheosis of all that was of good report; it is simply that in exercising its powers in those fields government behaved without that degree of specialness that constitutionalists require. Thus slighted in areas of substantive policy, constitutionalists fall back on procedure. At least, they are tempted to say, the procedures by which governments are held to account have been revised in ways that are consistent with the proposition that there is something peculiar about governmental powers. These claims are made both in relation to Parliament's procedures, and, most often, about the role of the courts.

As to Parliament, the main thrust of constitutionalism has been to stress the importance of Parliament's supposed role in holding governments accountable for their actions. To do this it has concentrated its fire on two matters; first, a quest for new meaning and strength for the doctrine of ministerial responsibility, and second, the promotion of a new scrutinising role for Parliament through the medium of select committees.

In neither case has much progress been made. Granted, select committees have, since the St John Stevas reforms of 1979, become the main locus (as compared, for example, with a sterile Question Time) for the serious scrutiny of government policy. Granted, too, they have been the medium by which information about the working of government, in quantities quite inconceivable two decades ago, has been opened to public debate. Conversely, those outside the government have been able to use the committees to put relatively heterodox views to government; this aspect of the committees as a two-way conduit has been useful. But there is no evidence that the relationship of power between government ministers and parliamentary backbenchers has been changed at all by select committees' work. As the government showed when replying to a request by the Treasury and Civil Service Committee to interview some of those civil servants most intimately involved in the Westland affair, ministers are perfectly capable of treating the new committees with something approaching contempt. Moreover, there is no evidence that select committees have, by the sheer quality of their work, convinced government to change a policy in a way which, absent the committee's intervention, it would not otherwise have countenanced.

Constitutionalists have had a particularly poor time of it in the field of ministerial responsibility. Some suggestions have an air of almost pathetic unreality. Consider the claim that there is something odd about organisations like the Manpower Services Commission, outwith direct ministerial control, such that if 'their civil servants operate autonomously from ministers, then they should be wound up'[4] – this at a time when the government appears to be seriously thinking of treating most of the public service in just this way.[5] Or take this proposition, 'Ministers who delegate decision-making authority and then do not accept responsibility are acting irresponsibly; they should be sacked',[6] this after the experience of all governments since (say) 1964. Time without number (consider Mr

Eric Varley rescuing Chrysler in 1975 just after publishing a White Paper in which he implied he would do no such thing; and various ministers for Northern Ireland, at various times, ducking responsibility for security catastrophes) politicians have demonstrated that the extent to which they will accept blame for the actions of their departments is a matter on which there are no guidelines of constitutional practice. Far more, it would seem, depends on what the prime minister of the day assumes is the right, or desirable, political resolution of the matter.

The disappointment of those who have argued that the growth of administrative law in Britain – and in particular the judicial review of administrative action – has advanced the cause of constitutionalism has been no less acute. Lord Diplock, one of the three or four judges most influential in this endeavour, has spoken of 'that progress towards a comprehensive system of administrative law that I regard as having been the greatest achievement of the English courts in my judicial lifetime'.[7] In terms of academic learning, perhaps even of the number of cases in the appellate courts, this may be so (though Maitland noted long ago that many of the cases in the nineteenth-century Law Reports concerned the proper exercise of public powers). But if, as has until recently been conventional to assume, it is considered that this 'growth' of administrative law has acted as a check on the power of government, recent research has exploded the myth.

Prosser has shown how easy it is to overturn a judicial decision that limits an administrator's discretion;[8] Hutchinson has said that the claims for administrative law as an instrument of control of government are no more than a 'ruse'.[9] Rawlings goes so far as to suggest that the very possibility of judicial review has given governments an opportunity to legitimate activity that in other circumstances would render them open to severe criticism.[10]

Quite possibly, some of this new revisionism is overdone. Even if later overturned by legislation, a finding by a court that a certain activity is illegitimate, or has been taken in a procedurally suspect way, establishes for the complainant a legal right to redress. No other institution in the British system can visit such a blow to the powerful. Yet the central message of the new learning is clear; neither in its principles (which have been allowed to get hopelessly woolly) nor in its impact (which, as De Smith said, is bound to be sporadic)[11] has judicial review satisfied its boosters' claims. It has provided neither a language nor a method for treating certain decisions with that degree of specialness that the constitutional perspective requires.

II

Why has constitutionalism failed? The overarching reason is that those asserting it have omitted, explicitly or implicitly, to stipulate a theory of the state. Dissatisfied with the current condition of the British constitution, with rare exceptions (of which utopian socialists are perhaps the most easily understood, if least relevant, example) they have been unable to tell their audience what alternatives they have in mind. This has been true for 'professional', academic constitutionalists, who have had little excuse, as it has been for the many members of the commentating class who have felt that Britain's system of government left much to be desired. It has been a crucial failing. The natural audience for those who have promoted constitutionalism has been those with power – a stake – in the existing system. The terrible tendency of the British to reduce everything to common-man practicalities has made it easy to ask of those who propose change: 'What would you put in its place?' When answers – when available – are discordant, the ascendancy can rest assured that it will not seriously have to justify its power.

Yet the failure to stipulate alternative theories of the state is understandable. It is an exercise fraught with difficulties imposed on constitutionalists by three, interconnected factors. The first is an uncertainty of aim. Those who have been committed to constitutionalism have never been clear – or perhaps have never dared to make clear – to what extent they were involved in a new but value-free examination of government, and to what extent they were concerned more than anything else with reform. As Murphy has suggested,[12] if modern constitutional scholarship allows itself to be nothing more than yet another forum for the criticism of Mrs Thatcher, it is worthless. Put another way, constitutionalism tends to be a cry of the powerless. The call for certain powers to be treated specially has become virtually indistinguishable from a call that they should be exercised sparingly. In modern Britain, constitutionalism speaks of a state of affairs not as it is but as how those who espouse it wish it to be. It is almost inevitably a critical theory. Those whom it is critical of are those who hold power; almost by definition those who have advanced it tend to be those opposed to the powerful. When in opposition, the Conservative laywer Lord Hailsham discovered an 'elective dictatorship', but forgot about it when Lord Chancellor. The Labour Party, when it tasted the bitter fruit of powerlessness during the 1980s, was happy to discover constitutional issues in the condition of local government, in the Ponting case, or in the behaviour of the Prime Minister during the Westland affair; not in its own use of prerogative powers to enforce a prices and incomes policy. Modern Britain has been a highly politicised country – a place where cleavages between people with different visions of the common good have, by standards in other mature democracies, been uncommonly deep. In these circumstances, it has been difficult for a politically value-neutral constitutionalism to emerge, and hence easy for the government of the day to dismiss the claims of those who assert constitutional specialness as a political attack ill-disguised as a principled one.

Secondly, even among those who are without political power for the time being, constitutionalism or the lack of it in the government of the day has been a second-order question. Political debate in Britain has been, primarily, about the control and distribution of economic largesse. The assumption by both main political parties has been that the important thing is the winning of power; that way they can distribute economic gains in the way that their preferences and ideologies incline. Within this framework, constitutionalism has been considered to be just a needless constraint on a greater good.

The Labour Party, for example, has consistently attacked the civil liberties record of Conservative governments. Yet it has no less consistently refused to commit itself to anything like a Bill of Rights designed to guarantee certain civil liberties. Instead, it has taken the view that the constraints in any such a Bill would be more trouble than they were worth. A Bill might, for example, protect private property, yet Labour might feel that the ability to confiscate such property (by nationalisation, or because it was against private education) outweighed the need for protection. Grant, in an attack on those who have argued for the need to look at local government from a constitutional perspective, has put this point of view with great clarity. The constitutional debate, he argues is a sterile one.[13] 'Because of its focus upon the formal relationship between government bodies, it threatens to overlook the broader grounds of recent central–local conflict. It is not purely conflict between institutions. It is conflict between a variety of economic and socio-political choices; between investment and consumption, between the public and the private sector, and between collective and individual welfare'. Once a debate is cast in those terms – and so debates in

Britain typically have been – the chance to argue that they should be discussed in a special, constitutional way, and that actions should be justified by reference to some special, timeless standards, quickly goes by the board.

Thirdly, the constitutional project failed to appreciate the central significance of the sovereignty of parliament in British governmental debate. Parliamentary sovereignty, for these purposes, can be given two distinct meanings, both of which have had devastating consequences for constitutionalism. The first, legal, meaning, is familiar enough; Parliament is omnicompetent. It can do anything except bind its successors, and there is no authority outwith Parliament that can say that what Parliament has done (so long as certain procedural requirements have been met) is in any sense illegitimate.

This is an immense blow to the central tenet of constitutionalism. In Britain, Parliament is the creature (it is facile to pretend otherwise) of those who exercise executive power for the time being. Without support in Parliament, executive power is meaningless. But this means that it is open to any government to decide – as, in the cases of civil liberties and the territorial dispersion of power, modern governments have indeed decided – that no question of specialness arises. As a matter of everyday activity the preferences of the government of the day are given a legally protected aura. It is this (and not, for example, the more lurid possibility of retrospective legislation, quite ordinary under the legal definition of sovereignty) that makes the constitutional project so difficult. Constitutionalism says that certain matters must be treated in a certain way and subject to timeless principles; politicians with a majority of one for the time being in the House of Commons say 'Phooey to that'. And the politicians have not just might, but right, on their side.

Moreover, the second sense of parliamentary sovereignty reinforces this position. This is the deeply-held belief in the British scheme of things that elected politicians should have a monopoly of power, and that political checks on them (presumably – there is a great deal of presumption here – meaning checks exercised by other politicians, or by election) are the ones that are most desirable. This doctrine is in some respects a curious one. It has, for example, made it virtually impossible to find any basis on which a civil servant might object to the policy of his minister, however outrageous. To do so would be for an appointed official to set himself above a political one, which would be unforgivable. It has been the source of much confusion in local government, offering local authorities a kind of spurious (and historically unfounded) legitimacy, however daft their actions, just because they happen to be elected.

Curious or not, it is no less damaging to the constitutional project than is the legal meaning of sovereignty. Constitutionalism must require that someone outwith those who exercise power has a hand in checking to see whether power has been exercised with the required degree of specialness. Yet to so establish centres of power (which would probably be judicial in form) runs straight into this second meaning of sovereignty. As Ridley has said, 'political rather than judicial control is a central feature of Britain's unwritten constitution'.[14]

III

The key question facing constitutionalists in 1988, and for the rest of the century, is whether the conditions of failure are as strong as ever. There are grounds for thinking that they are not.

If constitutionalism is to find new life, it will be because Britain's public life more generally is changing. At the heart of this change is a reassessment of the strength of sovereignty as the key determinant of constitutional and political realities. At first sight, this claim might be surprising; many public lawyers have ben expecting a reappraisal of sovereignty for 20 years, and have been disappointed. There were those who – rightly – thought that the devolution proposals of the 1970s would deal a death blow to Parliament's legally-protected omnicompetence. Under those proposals, legislative initiative was to be shared between the Westminster Parliament and the Scottish and Welsh assemblies, while, in a development which would have marked a new role for the courts, the Judicial Committee of the Privy Council was to be charged with considering the *vires* of legislation as measured against the terms of constitutive Acts. For others, the damage to sovereignty was supposed to come through adherence to the European Convention of Human Rights. As the convention produced more cases based on its terms, in both the institutions of the Council of Europe and in domestic courts, so it was thought that judges would grope their way to rendering void statutes inconsistent with the terms of the Convention. But devolution was shot down at the referendum-box, and the English courts have been uncertain in their attitudes to the European Convention. Neither development was enough to crack the wall of sovereignty.

To any significant extent, the same has been true in the third, and most important area where lawyers thought that sovereignty was bound to be challenged. This was in the field of Britain's treaty obligations to the European Community. There, the omnicompetence of Parliament seemed to run head-on against the Community's doctrine of the primacy of its own law.

With the benefit of hindsight, lawyers assumed too much in the early 1970s. They thought that the mere legal fact of a conflict between two theories of sovereignty would lead to an early challenge to the British one, and that British courts would soon have to come to terms both with a 'new legal order', and with a new place for themselves in it. That was always too formalistic, and looked only to the consequences of accession to the communities on the first – legal – form of sovereignty identified above.

It now seems plain that the real effect of accession to the Community has been to undermine the second, political sense of sovereignty; the sense that key decisions of the day should be taken by British politicians accountable to the institutions of British politics. This is not simply because – for example – more decisions are now to be taken in the Council by majority vote, and more powers arrogated by the European Parliament. To concentrate on those matters would be, once more, to confuse form for substance. The real changes depend on economic policy, especially when the single European market is manifested by the free movement of capital, labour and goods – a position that all Community members are committed to reaching by 1992. Once the internal market is fully in place, it will, for example, be impossible for all practical purposes for the British government to exercise complete freedom of action over its rates of indirect taxation. This impossibility will only partially be a function of the terms of the relevant British and Community laws; it will have much more to do with economics. So long as there is almost free movement of the factors of production, consumers will shop where they can get the best deal. A British government which (for example) tries to tax certain goods and services more heavily than they are taxed in France will find that sooner or later its merchants are losing business to French ones. Just as in the United States, taxes within the various territories of the European Community, while unlikely ever to be identical, will soon gravitate close to a mean.

This, plainly, will amount to a significant diminution of sovereignty. As it happens, without constitutional scholars noticing, the British government has for most of the 1980s (and certainly since the election of 1983) been acquiescing in a constraint no less significant. For by tying (without making such links explicit) the pound to movements within the European Monetary System, and in particular to the international level of the Deutschemark, British politicians have ceded a good deal of their instruments of economic policy (over interest rates, for example, and hence acceptable levels of inflation) to institutions or markets, outwith their direct control. The fact that, in the spring of 1988, the government seemed to take a new view on the appropriate level of the pound in relation to other currencies than it had hitherto does not destroy the case but makes it. It underlines that not just policy, but changes in policy, are to be fixed by reference to an external variable.

This significant surrender of sovereignty has been driven by technological change. Until the 1980s it was far easier to trade merchandise goods internationally than it was to trade capital. Twenty years ago international trade-flows of goods were considered far more worthy of attention than international capital flows. National governments hedged international capital dealings about with all sorts of regulations, while the technology to shift capital from one country to another instantaneously had not been developed. Within the memory of most of those reading this book, British governments were able to limit the amount of foreign exchange that an individual could spend outside the country to £50 a year. In a world without credit cards, or electronic funds transfers, that was plausible; it now seems to be quite incredible. Today, trade in merchandise goods is dwarfed by international flows of capital.

It would in principle be possible for a country to ignore these trends and seek to reestablish exchange controls. In a world economy ever more interdependent, however, it has become fantastically costly to do so. Countries that are open to the world's capital markets will be those to which international investment and hence prosperity will flow. And the policing of exchange and capital controls is, in a world of electronic currency dealing, far more difficult and expensive than most governments (that of Mexico, for special reasons, apart) have yet realised.

The consequence is that significant instruments of economic policy are now outwith the control of national governments, and will continue to be so for the foreseeable future. In Britain, this development has been compounded by another, itself also seen in other western countries. Crudely put, this is the collapse of the intellectual and political appeal of interventionist economic policy (a change linked to the internationalisation of capital, for capital is bound to flow to places where it will get the best return, which, other things being equal, will be market economies).

These twin developments are nowhere of such importance as in Britain. Here, perhaps more then anywhere else, divisions in politics since 1956 have been not about foreign policy but about competing visions of the economy. Signing up for one express or implied economic theory or another has been the way in which political loyalty has been defined.

This condition can only exist if distinct economic visions are plausibly on offer; at a time of European integration and the free international movement of capital, they cannot be. The British debate on economic policy is already being squashed into channels far narrower than seemed possible ten years ago. One consequence of this change has already been hinted at – it renders the classic case of the political sovereignty of Parliament redundant. There is much in economic policy that Parliament cannot now do. But secondly, the new and diminished politics of economic policy mean that the objection that constitutionalism is a second-order question for those seeking power looks dangerously weakened. Control of the first-order power – redistributive economic policies – is simply not as attractive as it used to be. Its tools have been blunted. Put another way, changes in the way in which economic policy will be discussed politically create room for a new kind of politics – one that concentrates on non-economic matters.

What will the new politics consist of? At the moment, any comments are bound to be of the most speculative sort. Some hints, however can be gleaned by the work of those within politics who have been most affected by the changes in economic climate – which means those to the left of the political centre. From the Labour Party (albeit from its revisionist wing; but then what part of it is not now revisionist?) have come suggestions that questions of liberty and empowerment will be critical to the coming political debate. The various parties competing for the political centre during the 1980s agree, and have placed these demands within a more explicit context of constitutionalism.

The obvious riposte is, 'So what?' Does this not reinforce the point that constitutionalism is a value espoused only by those who are powerless? Yet here, too, the ground may be shifting. It was a Conservative Member of Parliament who took the lead in the most successful attack yet made on the Official Secrets Act. Conservative politicians have expressed interest in the European Convention on Human Rights, and it is Conservative politicians (whether elected to the European Parliament, or appointed to the Commission) who have, wittingly or not, been the stormtroopers for an attack on parliamentary sovereignty from Brussels and Strasbourg.

At the very least, all three of the reasons for the failure of the constitutional project look weaker than they recently did. This does not mean that all debates about the proper exercise of power in modern Britain are henceforth to be cast in terms which all constitutionalists will understand, or that there will be a sudden consensus about the limits of that power. Britain will not, in the foreseeable future, and however much underlying political debate may change, give itself a constitutive document. There are two reasons for that. The first is that such documents almost invariably depend on a legal revolution – either the creation of a new state from the ashes of an old one (the German or French cases in the 1940s and 1950s) or a sundering of the ties with a colonial power (the American case among many others). No catastrophe of such a kind is in prospect for Britain. Secondly, any such constitutive document would almost invariably force Britain to engage in a national debate about the Crown and the nature of Monarchy. For under such a system, where would ultimate constitutional authority lie? With the Crown, dressed up comfortably, as it is now, as 'The Crown in Parliament'? Or with the Constitution? Such a debate remains the grand taboo of modern Britain.

The American experience is crucial here. Even with a politics which, by British lights, has long since demonstrated a degree of consensus on economic matters quite unknown this side of the Atlantic (there is no real political argument in America about its capitalist nature); even with a written constitution whose terms are honoured at every possible juncture, American constitutionalism does not demonstrate a face of bland consensus. For one thing, as Kammen[15] has shown in one of those rare books that is truly seminal, the terms of the constitution – including the Bill of Rights – are far from being widely known, much less understood. And the extent to which the constitution has been considered to be critical to American political debate has swung wildly from one extreme to another over the years.

Moreover, as the events of the last eight years in America have conclusively proved, a commitment to discussing certain matters within a constitutional framework emphatically does not mean that they are depoliticised. Behind the rejection by the Senate in 1987 of the nomination of Judge Robert Bork to a vacancy on the Supreme Court lay a fundamental disagreement – rooted firmly in partisan politics – about what the constitution is, and what role the judges have in applying and interpreting it in judicial causes. On the one hand are those who, crudely, believe that the constitution is a living document, whose terms are to be interpreted by judges in the light of the times in which they live. On the other, are those who believe that a judge's principal role should be to discover the original intent of those who framed certain constitutional words and phrases. To do otherwise (in a phrase associated with Bork that neatly illustrates how the role of American judges is not one on which there is a consensus) involves judges doing no more than to 'look into themselves'.

Nor does the fact of a written constitution, and a political consensus on the essential nature of a society, mean that the institutions of government are considered to be perfect. During the bicentennial year of the adoption of the American constitution in Philadelphia, the legislative and executive branches seemed to be paralysed in the face of a severe economic threat. Even after the awful warning of a stockmarket crash, measures to trim the federal budget deficit to within sustainable limits took two months to effect. Many American commentators have noted that the bifocation of power in Washington, with one party controlling the Presidency and another the Congress, can make rational, effective government terribly difficult. Others have noted a decline in party loyalty, and a hijacking of the national interest by the maxim that 'all politics is local'. Yet others have commented that the process of revising the constitution is more difficult than either Madison or Jefferson seemed to think it would be. Calls for reform of governmental processes are not a prerogative of those countries without a written constitution.

On the other hand, the lessons of America's commitment to constitutionalism can give heart to those committed to such a project in Britain. A commitment to limited government (through dividing powers three ways at the federal level, and territorially, between state and federal government) can make decision-making messily difficult, but also curiously exhilarating. Power divided really is (think of the 1987 Irangate hearings in Congress) power constrained. Rights once granted (think of the way the press has been able to use the First Amendment) are rights that will be continuously asserted. If the conditions that have led to the failure of constitutionalism in

Britain are weaker than they recently were, a more effective form of government may or may not result: on that, the evidence is bound to be inconclusive. But through the haze, it may just be possible to discern a healthier way in which the interests of the governed and the governing can be reconciled.

Notes

1. 'The Constitutional Dimension', *Public Administration*, 64, 1986, pp. 277, 278.
2. See my own *The Role of Law in Central–Local Relations*, SSRC, 1981; Grant, 'Central–Local Relations: The Balance of Power', in Jowell and Oliver (eds), *The Changing Constitution*, 1985, among many others.
3. Cornford, 'The Constitutional Dimension', op. cit., pp. 279–80.
4. Jones, 'An Answer: Stand up for Ministerial Responsibility', *Public Administration*, 65, 1987, pp. 87, 89.
5. *Improving Management in Government: The Next Steps*, Report to the Prime Minister, HMSO, 1988 (£3.90).
6. Evidence to Treasury and Civil Service Committee report on *Civil Servants and Ministers*, 1986, Vol. II, p. 296.
7. *R v. IRC, ex p. National Fed. of Self-Employed*, 1982 AC at 641.
8. 'Politics and Judicial Review', *Public Law*, 1979, p. 59.
9. 'The Rise and Ruse of Administrative Law and Scholarship', *Modern Law Review*, 1985, p. 293.
10. 'Judicial Review and the "control of government"', *Public Administration*, 64, 1986, p. 135.
11. *The Judicial Review of Administrative Action*, 4th ed., 1980.
12. Book Review, *Public Law*, 1986, p. 64.
13. Grant, 'Central–Local Relations', op. cit., p. 234.
14. 'The Citizen against Authority; British approaches to the redress of grievances', *Parliamentary Affairs*, 1984, p. 37.
15. *A Machine that Would Go of Itself*, Michael Kammen, h/back, Knopf, USA, 1986; p/back, London House, USA, 1987.

II Spreading Power

3 Change in Local Government

Nicholas Deakin

THE BACKGROUND

In the lengthy catalogue of grievances drawn up by his ungrateful former subjects shortly after his hasty departure for France, James II's repression of municipal corporations does not feature prominently. Nevertheless, it found its place on the roll of dishonour contained in the Declaration of Rights; and has generally been taken as typical of the attitudes of the Stuart Kings towards all those institutions that offered any form of systematic resistance to their concept of absolute rule.[1]

Like other institutions – the Church of England, the City companies, the universities – the corporations survived both James's malice and the torpor that descended upon all of them under his Hanoverian successors. In their reformed incarnation, after the Municipal Corporations Act of 1835, local authorities began a rapid – if uneven – expansion in the range of their activities. By mid-century, local government had become one of the institutions forming an integral part of the constellation of public bodies that made up the already far-from-minimal mid-Victorian State. This expansion was made possible in part by the enlistment of the energies and commitment of the middle class, especially the provincial bourgeoisie. This class, which has been greatly admired for the vigour of its commercial enterprise by commentators as various as Karl Marx and Margaret Thatcher, saw local government as a suitable vehicle for their civic ambitions: a concern that took visible shape in the great monuments of provincial public architecture of the period.[2]

For the Victorians, the rationale for this expansion of public action at local level took a variety of forms. In its most general form, it was based on their pervasive concern about the quality of public life and the implications of the expansion of the franchise and concomitant moves towards greater democracy. In a well-known passage in his essay *On Liberty*, John Stuart Mill roots the case for local institutions in their value as a means of civic education, for active citizens, 'accustoming them to the comprehension of joint interests, the management of joint concerns – habituating them to act from public or semi-public motives, and guide their conduct by aims that unite instead of isolating themselves from each other'.[3] A politician of the generation after Mill, the Conservative Prime Minister Lord Salisbury, made the case in a more pragmatic form, in defending his cabinet's decision to establish an elected authority for the capital, the future London County Council. His concern, too, was with a familiar constitutional theme, the notion of the importance of the maintenance of checks and balances within the state system. 'Now, bear in mind' (he told his party audience) 'what true reform of local government means. It does not only mean – which I quite admit – that the local authorities should be properly elected; but it means that when you have provided the proper constitution of local authority you must provide that the local authority must have sufficient powers; and that it gets these powers by diminishing the excessive and exaggerated powers that have been heaped on the central authorities in London.'[4]

But beyond these considerations, local government came increasingly to be seen as the efficient vehicle for new measures of social reform. This, of course, is a line most often associated with the Fabian Society in general, and the Webbs in particular, and illustrated in practice by the activities of the Progressive coalition in power on the London County Council, in whose activities Sidney Webb played such a prominent part. But it is important to stress that promotion of an active role of this kind for local government extended far beyond the ranks of the Fabians, and long predated their advocacy of 'gas and water socialism'. Joseph Chamberlain's Birmingham provides an earlier and in some senses more comprehensive example of municipal enterprise promoted through collective political action, by a member of the precisely that class retrospectively canonised by the present Prime Minister for their individual initiative. By the turn of the century, when the Liberal Sir William Harcourt (the 'singularly well-oiled weathercock', as the Fabian Hubert Bland called him) observed that 'we are all socialists now', it was this collectivist consensus to which he referred. This demonstrably broad acceptance of the legitimacy of collective action based on local initiatives predates the formal introduction of systematic welfare state legislation and enabled Webb himself to claim that 'the opening of the twentieth century finds us all, to the dismay of the oldfashioned Individualist, "thinking in communities"'.[5]

The steady expansion of the state's role in social policy that followed, and which was greatly accelerated by the First World War, was sustained in large measure by conferring additional powers and responsibilities on local government. The extent of the initiatives that had become open to an energetic local authority was famously illustrated by the range of activities initiated by the LCC after its capture in 1934 by the London Labour Party under Herbert Morrison's leadership. In the following year, a trio of constitutional luminaries – Harold Laski, Ivor Jennings and William Robson – reviewing the record of local government since the passage of the Municipal Corporations Act a century earlier, entitled their celebratory volume, without the faintest detectable shade of irony, *A Century of Municipal Progress*.[6] Progress, that is, founded on a strong sense of civic identity, and providing a legitimate counterweight to central power, based on the assumption and efficient discharge of a wide range of new functions.

More than half a century further on, the picture is entirely different. Local government, an authoritative independent commentator recently observed, is 'under siege'.[7] This is not merely a matter of local government's claims to have efficiently discharged its functions being contested; the basic legitimacy of its activities and even its continued existence are increasingly coming into question. One of the most striking features of this decline has been its rapidity. The local government reforms of the 1960s and 1970s created, after the fashion of the day, larger units of government which were given new sets of responsibilities, notably in areas like strategic planning, and were intended to enhance the significance of their role. But these new creations withered on the vine as the impact of the deterioration in national economic performance progressively deprived them of the control over resources essential to the effective performance of their new duties. At the same time, client dissatisfaction with the quality of established services and local authorities' style of management was taken up and exploited by critics of all shades of political opinion. Most significant of all, however, was the election in 1979 of an administration determined to reopen the argument about the roles and responsibilities of government, which had for long seemed settled and on which the legitimacy of much of the expanded activity of local government depended. As the new Prime Minister had put it when still in Opposition: 'a vital new debate is beginning, or perhaps an old debate is being renewed, about the proper role of government, the welfare state and the attitudes on which it rests'.[8]

Over the following years of Conservative government, the dilemma of local government, caught between the external pressures of increasingly tight control from the centre and the growing internal problems of local citizen discontent and the active disaffection of its own staff has become increasingly painful. Moreover, there are no signs that the siege is likely to be lifted.

THE INDICTMENT

Many of the current criticisms of the performance of local government over the past decade are summarised in the *Report on the Conduct of Local Authority Business* (The Widdicombe Report), published in 1986. This report needs to be read with some caution. This is partly because of the context in which it was produced – the Government's evident concern about the successful use of press publicity and advertising by local authorities to oppose central policy initiatives; and partly because its focus is narrower than that of earlier inquiries. To some extent, the verdicts that Widdicombe passes are victor's justice. Nevertheless, it provides a convenient punctuation point to set against the municipal triumphalism of Jennings, Laski and Robson fifty years earlier.

In presenting their initial appraisal of the state of local government, the Widdicombe Committee identifies its rationale as lying in three characteristics: the contribution that local government makes to pluralism; the means it provides for participation in the democratic process; and its responsiveness to the needs of local people.[9] Judged by these three criteria, the case for arguing that local government is in need of urgent attention certainly seems persuasive. Taking them in turn, whatever contribution local authorities may make to constitutional pluralism in theory has not been reflected in practice. As a counterweight to central power, on the lines sketched by Lord Salisbury, even the larger authorities have proved ineffective when confronted with such determined opponents as his Conservative successors. A head-on challenge, in the shape of the GLC's energetic campaign for its own survival, was eventually defeated (though not without anxious moments); and the marginally less ambitious project, of achieving and defending municipal socialism in one authority, has failed almost without exception wherever it has been tried. The alternative of conciliation and attempts to interest government in forms of partnership has appeared too late to carry any conviction. The balance has gone down decisively on the side of the centre.

On participation, the record has been hardly more convincing. Despite all the publicity sought and given to the conflicts that have raged over the past decade between central and local government, the population at large have obstinately refused to be mobilised. Claims that the GLC were able to overcome this apathy and enlist widespread support dwindle on closer examination to the results of a few opinion polls about the general principle of an elected authority for the capital; judged by the criterion that really counts, the participation of the electors through the ballot box, London remained apathetic throughout.[10] This apathy, which reflects a general level of participation in local government elections which is shamefully low by European standards[11] provides central government with one of their strongest arguments for repudiating the concept of local choice through the local democratic process. By their reasoning, which Widdicombe endorses, there is no local mandate to set alongside that conferred by a majority at a Parliamentary election.[12] The local electorate can be educated by participation, as Mill wishes; but in the process they must also learn the hard lesson that all real power resides at the centre.

The failure of the local electorate to participate on a substantial scale may reflect deficiencies in the third area identified by Widdicombe: the responsiveness of authorities to local needs. In its most elementary form, this implies an inability (for whatever reason) to deliver the goods – or, more properly, the services – in the form that their clients wish to have them. To the criticisms of bureaucratic inertia that became commonplace in the 1970s have been added the suggestion that, on the contrary, public bureaucracies (of which local authorities have been taken, not always fairly, as the prototypes) have become too active in promoting their own interests, as opposed to those of their users. This bureaucratic imperialism, according to its critics (notably the 'public choice' school)[13] can take a variety of forms: promotion of the career interests of the senior managers of the bureau; colonisation by professionals seeking to secure possession of their bases and extend the territory to which they control access; and manipulation of the system by public sector unions anxious to promote the material welfare of their members. The consequences of this process, as seen by these critics, has been to reinforce tendencies to managerial inefficiency that are already intrinsic to the system, with its lack of the discipline of the bottom line of profit (or loss); and to limit the range of choices that are open to local consumers.

A further criticism of the capacity of local government to be sufficiently responsive which would command support among those who might not necessarily endorse all the criticisms of excessive bureaucracy relates to its ability to innovate successfully. The record of the past decade provides some evidence of new departures on local government policies and practices, on both the left and right ends of the spectrum; but local government's critics would maintain that many of these have more style than substance. This weakness, if it is one, is linked to concern about the quality of local authority staff; the standard of new recruits, their working relationship, in certain cases, to elected members and the political processes and the very high rate of wastage among senior officers.

These criticisms, taken together, have helped to reinforce the perception that local government has ceased to be, in the word printed in bold type in the Widdicombe Report, 'effective' and thereby fails to satisfy the most important of the tests that its advocates at the turn of the century established: its ability to serve the public interest efficiently.

WHY HAS THE COUNTER-REVOLUTION SUCCEEDED?

If this indictment is a true bill, how has this situation come about, and so rapidly? Certainly, there is no mistaking the shift of power to the centre that has taken place; but this is only part of a broader process. In the course of asserting its control over the machinery of government and the apparatus of State power, the Thatcher Administration, like James II, has not always assigned a very high priority to taking a grip on local government and its activities. Disappointed Conservative politicians have been prone to refer to the present Government as a 'Treasury Government';[14] and it has certainly been the case that from the outset economic goals have been given clear priority over all others. In the process of asserting control over government activities and attempting (in practice, without striking success) to gain control over public expenditure, the Government has from the outset seen local authorities as part of the problem, not as potential partners in achieving solutions. The focus on resources and the controlling of the level and pattern of distribution within the public sector necessarily implied bringing local authorities, who are currently responsible for £30 billion of public expenditure (1986), under tighter control.

The milestones along this path are the local government legislation of the Heseltine period, in which the Government made repeated attempts to find a net with a sufficiently fine mesh to trap 'high-spending' authorities; the setting up of the Audit Commission (1982), with its brief to advise on securing economy, efficiency and effectiveness in local administration; and the invention of the poll tax (1987) as the device for putting a final end to local government's capacity to raise and spend substantial resources of its own on policies of its own devising. Add to that, as perhaps the clearest illustration of the Government's unwillingness to accept that municipal enterprise has a legitimate role to play in the economic revival of major cities, the creation of Urban Development Corporations, to take on the major responsibility for this role. In a state paper of uncertain status (*Action for the Inner Cities*, 1988), government could find no good word to say for local authorities and no responsibilities to confer on them; merely threats that, as one junior minister put it, 'incompetent or downright loony local authorities will be swept away'.[15]

But this shift to greater central control is not merely a flag of convenience on the voyage to economic recovery; it forms part of a still broader approach: a philosophy of government based on a stronger role for the State ('let no one say that we are a laissez-faire government; we are strong to do the things that have to be done', Margaret Thatcher, 1987) in combination with enhanced status for individuals and their expressed preferences. The crucial significance of the individual's choices lies in the form and location of its expression, through the market. As Richard Holme puts it: 'to categorise your fellow citizens primarily as consumers fits well with the mixture of social authoritarianism and individual economic competition which characterises Thatcherism'.[16] Herein lies the other main reason why local government and its main activities can find no comfortable place in the present government's scheme of things. The welfare state served, among its other purposes, as the great engine of expansion of local authority activity during the period of bipartisanship in the fifties and sixties. Now, it has come to exemplify all that the Prime Minister finds unacceptable about that period.

Latterly, the government's criticisms have come to focus particularly on two service areas under direct local control: housing and education. These, though not by any means the largest consumers of public funds, have come to form the front line in the ideological trench warfare between the government and its opponents. Local authority housing is taken by the present regime as a key example of an area where public provision could become redundant if the market were allowed to perform its natural function of making housing available at a cost and in a form that best suited the interests of both producer and consumer. There is widespread dissatisfaction at the standards of much of the local authority rented housing constructed during the fifties and sixties, most notoriously system-built high-rise apartment blocks; the style of management of some (not all) local authorities is taken as further evidence that the public sector is incapable of fulfilling this role; and the success of the government's programme of enforced sales of council housing is proof that there is a ready alternative to hand. Current legislation will finish off the job by transferring the remaining public stock to housing associations and new trusts; removal of rent control in the private sector will leave mortgage interest tax relief for owner-occupiers as the only remaining major distortion in the functioning of the market. If this programme is successfully completed, it will effectively eliminate one complete area of local government activity.

In the other main contested area, local government may prove more difficult to dislodge. Recognition of the significance of the state's role in education goes back further than in housing; one clear implication of the extension of the franchise was the need for an education system whose products would be competent not just as economic units but as citizens making choices about the future of their society. However, dissatisfaction about the content of state education and the implications of the extension of the comprehensive system provided one of the early base camps in the long march of the right to power; many of the concerns expressed in the successive Black Papers on education are still present in current ministerial pronouncements. The forthcoming legislation proposes to increase central control over the content of the curriculum, while allowing individual schools to opt out of direct control by local authorities. Once again, the combination of centralisation and enhancement of individual choices will squeeze out the local authority – the only custodian, however imperfect, of the collective interest.

The pattern that is being set in this way has been reinforced by constraints upon resources, which in turn lowers both the quality of the service and the morale of staff, an outcome that can then in turn be employed as a further rationale for fundamental change. Neither of the two most exposed local services commands the general level of public support that can still be mobilised for the National Health Service; although parental anxieties may yet prove an obstacle to the passage of the education legislation in its present form.

For the moment, however, it can be assumed that the current round of reforms will be implemented; and it is to the consequences of their implementation and the alternatives that remain for local government that I turn next.

TOWARDS ALTERNATIVES FOR LOCAL DEMOCRACY

As the tedious Irishman of legend suggested, designing an alternative system would be an altogether simpler task if only we did not have to start from where we are now – or more precisely, where we can expect to be at the end of the Government's present term of office. But if the exercise is to have any degree of credibility it is important to recognise that the clock cannot (and indeed should not) simply be put back.

By the time the neo-Liberal counter-revolution has run its course, local delivery of major services will be organised on an altogether different basis. On present trends, their distribution between public and private sector is likely to be quite uneven. Different services present different opportunities for contracting out and privatisation; local circumstances may also determine which policies are introduced in which sequence in any particular area. Central legislation will set the framework; nevertheless, experience is likely to vary quite widely. Some areas will have experienced public asset-stripping of the crudest sort, of the kind that has already taken place in certain London boroughs; others will have passed through a planned process of devolution of responsibilities to well-founded and funded voluntary organisations on the basis of contractual arrangements that have properly negotiated and will be kept under review. Superimposed on this variety of different forms will be the 'black holes' produced by the creation of Urban Development Corporations and the consequent loss of responsibilities by the local authorities affected. This unevenness is likely to persist for some time; although in the absence of a written constitution defining the limits of central power, the general trend towards loss of authority by the periphery is likely to develop an irresistible momentum, unless there is a fundamental change in the political landscape.

But other changes, not directly produced by government policies towards the public sector, will also alter the context in which new policies have to be devised. The revival in the economy, by stimulating consumer demand, will also stimulate consciousness of the scope for choice and encourage comparisons of quality of service between sectors. The edge of these comparisons will be further sharpened by technological developments, notably easier access to a wider range of information.

At the same time, the unevenness of the recovery has left some marked discrepancies of outcome; not only the different experiences of different geographical areas – not just the notorious North–South divide, part fact, part imaginative journalism – but a widening gap between rich and poor, to which many commentators have recently drawn attention.[17] Unless the gap starts to close in the later stages of the present government's term of office, it is likely to come to coincide more and more closely with another gap to which J. K. Galbraith first drew attention thirty years ago, between private affluence and public squalor.[18] Poor-quality public services for poor people contrasting with variety and choice for the prosperous majority; it is not hard to image the American experience being transposed to Britain by the end of the century.

In considering how best to respond in such circumstances, three broad alternatives seem worth considering. Following the Layfield Report on Local Government Finance (1976),[19] I shall call two of these *centralist* and *localist.* The third I would term *pluralist.*

The case for *centralist* solutions must now be even stronger than it was a decade ago. Although a wholly centralised system would be unusual in a country the size of the United Kingdom, it is perfectly feasible, as Widdicombe pointed out, to combine strong central control over policy and resource allocation with a devolved system of local administration. This would be progressively simpler to manage as an increasing number of functions once performed by public agencies are purchased on an individual basis in the market. Those collective services that still need to be formally provided can be organised by making the residual local executive agencies – either those in the public sector or private bodies to whom responsibilities have been contracted out – directly accountable to existing central government Departments. Alternatively, following the recent Efficiency Unit report on the Civil Service,[20] they could be managed by creating new freestanding subordinate agencies. Models for these already exist in the UDCs and in the plethora of quangoes created to manage London's affairs after the demise of the GLC. To the extent that some form of local identification is required, this can be achieved either by the appointment of local worthies of appropriate political complexion to the Boards that have been created; or by permitting a measure of democratic input by the direct election of a Mayor or Leader to act as a representative of local opinion and spokesperson on those policy issues on which the centre chooses to consult the periphery formally.

This model may, perhaps, appear excessively crude; but the broad lines are consistent with the logic of the approach of the present government, and more particularly that of the current Secretary of State for the Environment, Nicholas Ridley.

The *localist* approach, as its name implies, starts from the opposite premise, that it is the role of the periphery that needs to be strengthened. It has been sketched out in the Layfield report; and latterly developed in more detail by Professors Stewart and Jones.[21] In its purest form, it consists not merely of a case for retention of existing services under local democratic control, but for capturing – or in some cases recapturing – the local services now managed by agencies of central government. (The most obvious example is the Health Service). To this should be added some of the new policy areas that have been developed by local authorities over the past decade and about which the present government have expressed such scepticism (local economic development would be an example here).

The case for this transfer would rest on two separate but linked arguments; first, that by being managed at local level and subject to local political control services will become more responsive to local needs; and, second that a public service orientation could be developed (or revived) which can effectively meet individual as well as collective interests. Evidence from experiments currently underway in Sweden suggest that the absence of the bottom line of profit does not necessarily adversely affect either staff motivation or quality of service.[22]

However, localist solutions face three major difficulties. First, and in the light of the experience of the past few years, crucially, there is the problem of securing direct control over resources. The Layfield solution to this difficulty was the creation of a local income tax; apart from the negligible problem of convincing the Treasury of the appropriateness of such a measure, such a tax would probably be unpopular – though whether it would be more unpopular than the poll tax remains to be seen.

A second major difficulty, to which the Widdicombe report devotes a great deal of attention, is the question of the compatibility between national policy objectives and local preferences expressed by strong local units of government. Any conflicts that might arise – for example with national economic priorities – must, according to Widdicombe, be resolved in favour of those national policies, since constitutionally local authorities only exist within the terms laid down centrally, and have only those powers that the centre is prepared explicitly to concede. However, to say this may be no more than to identify a constitutional issue; and one which, as the British architects of the West German federal constitution have proved, is capable of being resolved within the framework of a modern state apparatus. It is, however, evident from experience there and with other more recent experiments with federal schemes in France and Italy that the units of local government identified need to be of sufficient size and to attract politicians of sufficient calibre to provide a sufficiently strong counterweight to balance the ever-growing attractions of the metropolis. In short, we may be talking here about regional, not local government.

Finally, and more basically, it may well be that the developments described earlier have already gone far enough to make a localist solution of the kind described impractical. In a recent paper,[23] Howard Davies of the Audit Commission has calculated that by 1992 (the year by which the present Government's term of office must expire) on present policies alone, local government will have lost 37 per cent of its present staff and its levels of expenditure will have been reduced by 35 per cent.

The final, *pluralist* alternative is based on a recognition of the inevitability of these developments and sketches a new approach to meet these new circumstances. In the place of a local authority concerned with the delivery of services, it postulates local elected bodies which would have responsibility for setting policy priorities for all public agencies in their area and all those performing delegated functions under statutory authority outside the public sector. This planning responsibility would be reinforced by executive responsibility for distribution of resources allocated by formula from the centre as a block grant to the locality. The elected authority would act as advocate to central government both in relation to resource distribution and on strategic planning issues.

Although this kind of authority would lack direct executive functions outside those of planning and resource allocation, it would be responsible for managing contracts with private sector agencies; and might on occasion be responsible for setting up consortia to provide alternatives to existing services. These would be likely to be one-function agencies, possibly with a limited lifespan; and the local authority would not act as employer. The objective would be to ensure that as far as possible, the local consumer had variety and choice in services while maintaining standards and ensuring that statutory obligations are met. Such a model is untried and runs against the grain of the public sector tradition as it has developed in this country; but it is not necessarily incompatible with its broad objectives.

CONCLUSIONS

One way of assessing the alternatives is to explore how well they fit the criteria laid down by the Widdicombe Committee. If examined on this basis, the centralist alternative seems the least convincing. The contribution made by this approach to the balance of power between centre and periphery is by definition minimal, since centralising washes out any concept of countervailing power. Nor is centralisation likely to make a substantial contribution to local participation. The major gain is likely to be in the area of efficiency; and this would be achieved at the expense of democracy, a tradeoff explicitly repudiated by Widdicombe.[24] On the other hand, a system that depended heavily on the satisfaction of needs in the market could, if effective, extend responsiveness by increasing choice. It would also be the least costly, if cost is assessed only in terms of public expenditure.

The localist solution, by contrast, must satisfy the Widdicombe criterion of creating a viable counterweight to central power or fail in its main objective. The concern here would be with the other two criteria. The potential, at least, for participation would exist under a localist scheme; but the failure of the Metropolitan Counties – and to some extent the GLC – to enlist public attention and concern stands as a warning that merely to extend the size and range of functions of local authorities is no guarantee that involvement would increase. Here, and to some extent on the efficiency criterion as well, there are arguments that point in the other direction, towards decentralisation and neighbourhood level organisations. The experience of decentralisation in local government is already quite extensive; although exaggerated claims have at times been made, it does suggest that the potential for creating arrangements for service delivery that are more responsive and attract active participation by local people is considerable.[25]

The pluralist solution also seeks to square the circle by combining efficiency and democracy; the major problem of implementation (which is true to a greater extent of the localist solution) is that it envisages a voluntary surrender of control by the centre over the content of resource allocation decisions. The history of the past decade is of the Treasury asserting its control over public expenditure to an extent that has no parallel in a peacetime administration. Some things cannot be unlearned; and, given what we know about the nature of that institution, it is unlikely that it would wish to unlearn them. This would hold good whatever the political complexion of the party in power might be.

If that were not enough, the pluralist solution also envisages a fundamental change in the character of local government, from service provider to supervisor and contractor. Under the present government's legislation some experience of these new roles is already being accumulated; but if the pattern is to be firmly established local government will need reliable partners, not only in the private sector but among voluntary organisations. There is a risk here of too easily assuming both consent and competence. Privatisation has attracted its fair share of cowboys; but their failings have been well enough publicised and the means of dealing with them are sufficiently well known to ensure that any authority that is taken for a ride does so by choice.

The position on voluntary organisations is more complex. It is of the nature of voluntarism that skills and capacity are unevenly distributed and individual organisations march to the sound of half a dozen different drummers. This is as it should be; but it severely limits the scope for laying down uniform standards. Flexibility and local variation is not an option but a necessity.

A further major issue in a pluralist solution is the extent to which any new form of organisations would be explicitly political, or how far they are perceived as performing technical functions outside the partisan arena of local politics. If they are to achieve local acceptance, they cannot escape becoming part of the local political process. But an approach would be needed in which objectives were kept firmly in view; and some, at least, of the traditional players (the public sector unions, for example) would either be missing from the field altogether or performing in a very attenuated role.

On the Widdicombe criteria, then, a plausible case can be made for either of the latter two approaches, the localist and the pluralist. But it may be that these are not the grounds on which to reach conclusions, however hypothetical and tentative.

Viewed from the point of view of the future users of public services, it simply may not be sensible to search for preferences for one form of solution over another. Choices may vary over time and between services. In some cases, impersonal efficiency or market exchange may be the preferred mode: in others, the human response or a continuing relationship – possibly even an exchange – with the provider of the service. Building collective forms of popular participation may be a wholly appropriate exercise in some cases; but so may the creation of a service that focuses on a quick and effective response to the expressed needs of individuals (and their families, as the Prime Minister would certainly have us add). In certain circumstances, a sense of common purpose – even a common identity – can crystallise round a public service; but identifying the conditions in which this can come about is a difficult exercise: some highly self-conscious campaigns using all the techniques of modern marketing have ended in embarrassing failure.

Perhaps the only clear conclusion possible is that, in order to survive as local government into the twenty-first century, authorities will have to satisfy the minimum test: that is, to ensure that the services for which they are responsible are locally-rooted, responsive to user-preferences and cost-efficient. Merely to achieve this much would not in itself serve to lift the siege; but it would provide the essential base on which the more ambitious structures can then be constructed.

Notes

1. G. N. Clark, *The Later Stuarts*, Oxford University Press, Oxford, 1955.
2. Asa Briggs, *Victorian Cities*, Penguin Books, Harmondsworth, 1963.
3. J. S. Mill, *On Liberty*, Penguin Classics, Harmondsworth, 1968.
4. K. Young and P. L. Garside, *Metropolitan London*, Edward Arnold, London, 1982.
5. Sidney Webb, quoted in D. Read, *Edwardian England*, Harrap, London, 1972.

6. I. Jennings, H. Laski and W. Robson, *A Century of Municipal Progress*, Allen & Unwin, London, 1935.
7. Howard J. Davies: 'Local Government Under Siege' in *Public Administration*, Vol. 66, no. 1, Spring 1988.
8. Margaret Thatcher, *Let Our Children Grow Tall*, CPS, London, 1977.
9. *Report of the Committee of Inquiry into The Conduct of Local Authority Business* (The Widdicombe Report), Cmnd 9797, HMSO, London, 1986.
10. Chris Husbands, 'Local Authority elections in London, 1982–6' in *The London Journal*, Vol. 12, no. 2, Autumn 1987.
11. Widdicombe Report, op. cit., para. 2.73.
12. Ibid., para. 2.77.
13. A convenient summary of these views is Jane Shaw, 'James Buchanan and Public-Choice Economics', *Dialogue*, 77, 1987.
14. Cf. Francis Pym, *The Politics of Consent*, Sphere, London, 1985.
15. Quoted in Davies, 'Local Government Under Siege', op. cit.
16. Richard Holme, *The People's Kingdom*, The Bodley Head, London, 1987.
17. Alan Walker (ed.), *Divided Britain*, Child Poverty Action Group, London, 1987.
18. J. K. Galbraith, *The Affluent Society*, Hamish Hamilton, London, 1958.
19. *Paying for Local Government* (The Layfield Report), Cmnd 9714, 1976.
20. Efficiency Unit, *Improving Management in Government: The Next Steps*, HMSO, London, 1988.
21. George Jones and John Stewart, *The Case for Local Government*, Allen & Unwin, London, 1983.
22. Lennart Gustafsson, 'Renewal of the public sector in Sweden', *Public Administration*, vol. 65, no. 2, Summer 1987.
23. Davies, 'Local Government Under Siege', op. cit.
24. Widdicombe Report, op. cit., para. 3.48.
25. Paul Hoggett and Richard Hambleton (eds), *Decentralisation and Democracy*, SAUS, Bristol, 1987.

4 Sovereignty, Centralism and Devolution

Bernard Crick

In my *The Reform of Parliament* of 1964 I argued with some vigour the simple thesis that the power of the government machine had increased so much that the powers of Parliament needed a commensurate increase. This increase was not to threaten an elected government, but to hold it accountable, to force it to think again about its measures, sometimes to amend them, and to open up both the policy-making process and administration to greater publicity. Specialised committees seemed the key to the matter, a scarcely original view even then. What was original (or perverse) was the attempt to combine two theories often thought to contradict each other: an Hobbesian view of sovereignty and a Millite democratic theory of consent. 'Strong governments need strong opposition', I argued; and further that the strongest governments are those who can best mobilise consent. I assumed that the consent would always be that of a majority of the electorate – well, more or less. It was joy to be young and to have one's cake and eat it. I took a tough-minded view of the electoral system. 'Governments must govern' (did the Iron Duke say that or Dick Crossman?) etc.: indeed I coined a glib phrase that gained some currency, 'Parliament is a continuous election campaign': such was the fundamental mechanism that protected our basic liberties, etc., not any constitutional fine print.

In other words, there was no conflict between the theory of the sovereignty of Parliament and liberty so long as a few minor adjustments were made (with plenty of rhetoric to make reforms of parliamentary procedure sound ever so important) and the informal rules of the parliamentary game were still adhered to strictly. The constitution was, and should be, what those who wanted to practise parliamentary politics agreed among themselves were the rules needed to play the great game. Had not Jennings amended Dicey to the effect that the conventions of the constitution are simply the informal understandings needed to work the constitution, as it is?[1] It was an ingenious attempt to blend consensus theory with conflict theory – ingenuous I now think.

The mature wisdom of age need not blush for the follies of youth, but it can acknowledge them. Perhaps the theory was always self-contradictory. The Hobbists knew that given even a narrow parliamentary majority and a strong nerve, there were no restraints except (Britain being Britain) the next General Election and the relative unlikelihood of a government abolishing elections, except in time of national emergency. The timing was always fair game, as was a mild Callaghanesque chicanery over Boundary Commissions which, like adjusting the bases of unemployment and health statistics, were thought unlikely to lead to riot or rebellion. And Whigs or old Liberals knew that self-restraint and custom in the majority party in the House presented what Lord Hailsham, in Labour times, was to call 'elective despotism' – words he never even ate but simply ignored when Tory times came back again and even he became a bellman for Mrs Thatcher's elective despotism. And after the Falklands War we can never again all be sure to agree what is a state of 'national emergency' in which normal liberties can be suspended.

THE DECLINE OF INFORMAL RESTRAINTS

Or perhaps I have changed my mind simply because of events – as Beatrice Webb said of the rationalist Herbert Spencer, his only idea of tragedy was that of a theory killed by a fact. But changed it I have. The year of the abolition of the GLC, the prosecution of Ponting, and of the Westland affair changed my mind very rapidly, and not just on the one point that Parliament itself now seems an ineffective restraint on what our ancestors called arbitrary government. All these things, indeed, the protection of fundamental rights, the power of Parliament against the Government, electoral reform, freedom of information, the restoration and enhancement of local government, hang together. Being an intellectual, I can change my mind more rapidly than politicians: the broad alternatives for Britain were always there as a mental speculation, and as a known fact about so many other democracies.

My party leaders still pin their hopes in a working majority and total victory next time after one more great push, and show little interest in constitutional reform. But the surviving 'free spirits' (a phrase of Mill's) in the Labour Party – that is, those who are thoughtful and are not creeping for jobs in a future government (or the old days back again of the 'Think Tank' and political advisorships –

the academics on working holidays) – most of them are now at least fellow-travellers of constitutional reform. In the austere pages of *Marxism Today* and in the *New Statesman* these issues are openly discussed, even if party funding was withdrawn from *New Socialist* and the editor was sacked when, during the last General Election, he put the case for tactical voting rather than for blind faith, heroism and total loyalty. Hardly anyone in the Labour Party who uses their intelligence freely does not now believe that constitutional reform is a major issue. For rather different reasons, reformers in Eastern Europe, even in Russia, as well as Eurocommunists, are now writing seriously about constitutional law, something once very peripheral to the socialist enterprise in so far as it wasn't simply denounced as a bourgeois restraint on a united working class movement.

The old informal restraints are withering. One mourns as well as mocks. After all, the parliamentary effectiveness of the Opposition largely depended on them. The old Conservative culture of the gentlemen in politics, how Baldwin socialised MacDonald and the very ambiance of the House, among so many other examples, has given way to that of the power-hungry careerist. The political manners of the Tebbits, the Heseltines and the Lawsons now set the example. And much the same has happened in the civil service: its old sense of itself as a state within a state or as a 'corporation' (*Gemeinschaft*) of servants of the crown, against which we all protested, has given way to collective greed (the incredible *job* of the non-contributory inflation-proofed pensions) and an individualistic clamour for advancement, which has made them a soft target for politicisation.

There is now no majority of backbenchers on the 1922 Committee who care to tell the Prime Minister or even the Leader of the House that this 'will not do' or 'is not done': there is only a majority waiting for the call to minor office. The new breed simply don't know the old customs and have, unlike the old Tories, very little interest in history. Not to put too fine a point on it, they are often historically ignorant. The Left of the Labour Party used to bewail how 'the House' socialised the socialism out of Labour MPs. I've always doubted that – Ralph Milliband's unhappily influential *Parliamentary Socialism* was built on the dubious assumptions that if you don't drink out of a saucer you can't be serious, and that most Labour MPs started as Belgian revolutionary socialists rather than as British trade unionists. But it certainly socialised them into a belief in proceeding in a parliamentary manner, if they didn't believe that already, which was all to the good; but also into a belief in the sovereignty of Parliament (if only it were, after that next big push, in the right hands). There was no difference between a Herbert Morrison and Michael Foot on that score, nor is there between Tony Benn and Brian Gould. This is the heart of the problem.

Put it another way. The idea that there is a consensus of values has gone. I have long argued (since the first edition of my *In Defence of Politics* in 1962) that representative democracy does not need a consensus on *substantive values* at all, indeed it is itself a device for governing in a civilised manner societies with differing values. In Britain we have never had a consensus of values if we take differences of religious and political doctrines as seriously as their rival claims truly deserve; but we do need consensus on *procedural values*. We do not need to agree on *what* decisions should be made but only on *how* decisions should be made. After the London Government Act and the abandonment of Royal Commissions and interparty conferences as the established way of proceeding on major institutional or constitutional issues like local government powers and Health Service finances, any procedural consensus has plainly gone. The Government now habitually changes national institutions as if it assumes, from the purely political contingency of a divided Opposition, that re-election is as certain as the resurrection of the body after death. In formal terms of political theory the government has become the state. Small wonder that she speaks of 'my Ministers'.

I make my conversion from 'sovereignty of Parliament' to constitutionalism sound too rational. In fact a wild memory keeps intruding into my mind. Two years ago Norman Tebbit, when a cabinet minister and chairman of the Conservative Party, was addressing a Sixth Form Conference in Central Hall, Westminster. His typed speech was statesmanlike and mild in tone and quite Burkean in content, almost boring; it was the week of the pre-election suspension of monetarism. But the first question roused the sleeping Adam. A girl asked him: 'What is the Government going to do about AIDS?' He leapt to the edge of the platform, pointed his forefinger high in the air, 'What is *the Government* going to do about it, *you* ask *me*?', he shouted, 'I ask *you* what are *you* going to do about it!' About half the hitherto quiet and well-behaved audience jumped up and cheered, the other half howled and hissed with anger. What shocked me was that he did it deliberately and so skilfully: seeking to raise emotion on such a complex and sensitive issue, seeking to divide, seeking to destroy consensus, seeking to heighten disagreements, only wanting to excite supporters – the rest of our fellow-citizens could go hang. He had an unexpectedly persuasive effect on the chairman. He helped me think again about the second part of the great perennial equation: what to do with government power for the public good and how to restrain government power for the public good. I can remember, of course, some orators in my own party who would say things designed only to have a similar affect on Tories.

SOVEREIGNTY AND CENTRALISM

For the welfare of the country and the relief of unemployment and poverty, one should not want less power in the hands of public authorities, but it would be better were it more dispersed: and dispersed on a basis of an agreement that could outlast changes of government.

Parliament was once closer to tackling this problem than now. A resolution of the House of Commons of 4 June 1919 set up a Speaker's Conference on Devolution:

> That with a view to enabling the Imperial Parliament to devote more attention to the general interests of the United Kingdom . . . this House is of the opinion that the time has come for the creation of subordinate legislatures within the United Kingdom, and that to this end the Government . . . should forthwith appoint a Parliamentary body to consider and report –
> (1) upon a measure of Federal Devolution applicable to England, Scotland and Ireland, defined . . . by existing differences in law and administration. . . .
> (2) upon the extent to which these differences are applicable to Welsh conditions and requirements. . . .

To the surprise of Lloyd George, who expected it to fail easily, the conference readily reached agreement on the powers, areas and finances of devolved or subsidiary legislatures, but the parties were unable to agree about composition, whether nominated or elected assemblies, and if so how. In those immediate postwar days there were an appreciable number of Tory advocates of 'Home Rule All Round', so long as it was all round and not just limited to Ireland.[2]

After the Government of Ireland Act 1920, discussions of federalism or devolution vanished from British politics, certainly in Conservative and Labour ranks. The Irish question had, of course, finally been put to rest. In days when for so long it dominated British politics, public men had to do a great deal of constitutional thinking, and bargaining. A few of those skills were still there to be applied to decolonisation after 1945, although in the main the drafting of the new constitutions was a Colonial Office matter that followed closely precedents in the Old Dominions. (Note, in passing, that the Mother of Parliaments, allegedly wedded for life to Sovereignty, yet had cheerfully accepted, indeed often actively fermented, Federal promiscuity and pluralism among her older sons and daughters – young New Zealand actually had to resist federalism being thrust upon her.) But by 1974 when a Labour government found the need to conciliate Scottish nationalism, there was a lack of experience and an incapacity in constitutional thinking both in Westminster and Whitehall. It was grimly apparent in the clumsy drafting of the Scotland and Wales Bills of 1978 and in the lack of any clear line of logic or principle in the drafting instructions.

Vernon Bogdanor headed his study of those Acts with a quotation from Lord McDermott: 'As a nation the British have no great interest in either the institutions or the principles of law which determine the structure of their society and the means whereby it may change or develop.'[3] Only the Liberal Party had kept up the older tradition of constitutional thought.[4] Yet this could be changing. And if so 'the credit must go to Mrs Thatcher', Antony Wright has written; 'the Thatcher Government has provided a lesson in the nature and extent of concentrated executive power available to a majority party in Britain. As such it had provided a constitutional education for the Left.'[5]

Yet this 'education' may have to carry us very far: to question the need for the doctrine of 'sovereignty of Parliament' at all, or certainly to prevent it being confused with the basic idea of an effective state. The state could actually be stronger, in its ability to get things done and respond to people's expressed needs, if it was decentralised. There are two modes of power, as Bertrand Russell once argued: power as unchallengeability (it must be done by me or through this office, or not at all) and power as the ability to carry out premeditated intentions. On this analysis, over-centralised power, sometimes, indeed, the powers of the Prime Minister, can often frustrate intentions to get things done. (That is the theoretical explanation of the weakness of government under Wilson's idea of strong government.) The idea of sovereignty as unchallengeable and effective power, however, cuts very deep into the consciousness of even those English politicians who believe themselves to be purely practical men and women, almost proud of not having an idea in their heads: at least not abstract ideas like sovereignty. And yet even thinking politicians, like Enoch Powell on the one hand, or Michael Foot and Peter Shore on the other, were convinced that we had lost our sovereignty on the day or night of our accession to the EEC in 1970, although somehow we muddle on.

SOVEREIGNTY AS WHIG IDEOLOGY

The doctrine of the sovereignty of Parliament arose not just in opposition to the prerogative powers of the Crown in the post-1688 settlement, but because after the Act of Union of 1707 (still called Treaty of Union in Scotland) Parliament could deny that any legislation could have the force of law coming from any body other than itself: and also claim that there were no controls on its own legislation.[6] Blackstone asserted in his *Commentaries on the Laws of England* that:

> Parliament has sovereign and uncontrollable authority in the making, confirming, enlarging, restraining, abrogating, repealing, reviving and expounding of laws, concerning all matters . . . : this being the place where that absolute power, which must in all governments reside somewhere, is entrusted by the constitution of these kingdoms. . . . It can change and create afresh even the constitution of the kingdom and Parliaments themselves: as was done by the Act of Union and by the several statutes for triennial and septennial elections. It can, in short, do everything that is not naturally impossible.

But is there really such an absolute power? Only in a legal sense; no other body can make enactments. But Blackstone tells us nothing about what parliaments or governments in general can do, still less specific ones. That is an empirical and political matter. Blackstone makes a sound point about jurisdictions but offers a very dubious pseudo-empirical generalisation that 'absolute power . . . must in all government reside somewhere.' In the sense that there could be held to be an absolute quantum of power, it may very well be dispersed (and in some situations the more effective for that). The young Bentham in his *Fragment on Government* of 1776 mocked Blackstone.

Did he think that 'the Switzers lack government?' (Some Tories long suspected, after 1787, that 'these United States' were really an anarchy, or about to collapse for a clear lack of central sovereignty). And in the cases where power is in fact found in one place that does not ensure that it is absolute.

There is more than a whiff of rhetoric and of ideology in Blackstone's celebrated passage. It was meant to impress and overawe, just as Hobbes's picture of the state as 'Leviathan' – 'that mortal God' – was meant to frighten rational men into obedience, to stop all that destructive quibbling about 'conscience' that had led to the Civil War – 'the worm within the entrails of the body Commonwealth.' But no contemporary was so foolish as to think that it gave free rein to a useable absolute power. The political context of the popularisation of the lawyers' and philosophers' doctrine of sovereignty needs to be remembered. Parliamentary sovereignty was invoked for two great purposes: to *limit* the powers of the Crown, when some of that power was still desperately needed for the defence of the realm and the Protestant religion; and then to hold the new United Kingdom (as it was called after 1707) together. Roughly speaking 'sovereignty of Parliament' meant to lowland Scots a guarantee of law and order and the absence of anarchy, or in more *hamely* terms a reasonable hope to die in bed and not from sword-edge or musketball, fighting Catholic highlanders or Irish mercenaries on moss, moor or mountainside.

The Scottish Parliament was not widely venerated as the *national* institution – that belief came from nineteenth-century historians. Its career had been spasmodic and its composition was anything but popular. Yet the bargain it struck for the merger or takeover was a sensible and a stern assertion of national interest: free trade within all British possessions, the retention of Scotch law and Scottish lawyers – and, above all, bitterly resisted in the English House of Lords, the establishment of the Kirk as the Church of Scotland. The Kirk was far more representative of the common people than either Parliament, and remained so until this century. And the famous Scottish education system grew up after the Act of Union.

According to the pure theory of sovereignty the new United Kingdom Parliament could in 1708 or any time afterwards have legislated all these peculiar Scottish institutions into oblivion; but in practice this was impossible. The Highland clans were brutally repressed after the 1745 Jacobite rebellion, but there were more Scottish soldiers than English or Hanoverian in the Union army at

Culloden. Scotland flourished and flowered in the eighteenth century, apart from the Gaelic areas, both economically and culturally. But for three generations it was not forgotten in Westminster that a barbarian army with foreign support had got as far south as Manchester. In George IV's reign a deliberate government policy was launched to conciliate and reconcile for ever even the highlands. An official cult of 'Bonnie Scotland' was launched, by an English cabinet employing Sir Walter Scott as impresario. The King was sent North and he wore the newly unbanned kilt (to the clamorous delight of caricaturists in the golden age of that great art) once. So even in the 1830s conciliating Scotland was still seen as a political imperative.

In other words, when we became, or attempted to be, 'the United Kingdom', the major perennial problem of imperial politics from 1688 to 1920 became that of holding the United Kingdom together. The doctrine of parliamentary sovereignty was the English ideology of unity. There is a story of power, coercion and English arrogance, as in the highland clearances, the abolition of the Irish Parliament in 1800 and the successive Coercion Acts, indeed acts of coercion. But there is an equally real story of politics, conciliation and English tolerance, as in the restraint of sovereignty, the removal of Catholic disabilities, administration in Ireland according to local customs and increasingly in local hands. Scottish, Welsh and Irish national sentiments were celebrated, in song and story, a romantic interest in the Celtic lands became a kind of cultural politics. Unlike everywhere else in Europe the English did not develop a literature of nationalism – which would have been politically divisive. They developed instead a literature of imperialism in which, as in the tales of Kipling, representatives of each of the nations of the British Isles played their part – much as Shakespeare had portrayed in his scene of the army on the eve of Agincourt, a common soldier from each nation of these islands.

Perhaps it was these strategies that led the French to see in us a paradoxical propensity for both tolerance and perfidy. These policies failed in Ireland but succeeded in Wales and Scotland. The old English governing class were historically-minded and had considerable knowledge, strengthened indeed by landowning interest, of Ireland and Scotland. Our present masters are largely ignorant and dismissive of the territorial politics of the United Kingdom, are Anglocentric in mentality and Home-Counties suburban or mid-Atlantic in culture.

The Scots have continued to manage their own affairs. So much so that most lawyers and civil servants, in effect the Scottish establishment after the decline of the Kirk's authority, had little enthusiasm to have a democratic assembly placed over them according to the 1978 Act, even if it gave them new powers. But the decline of the Kirk exposed the lack of a clear national institution that could speak for Scotland, a quite unexpected consequence of the Act of Union; and rougher elements in that land, the majority, are not inclined to accept the implicit view of the Society of Advocates and the civil servants of St Andrew's House that they are 'auld Scotland to the life'.

Wales, the most assimilated and least troublesome part of the United Kingdom to England, gained numerous concessions, touching religion, language, education and local government, not only in the national revival of the second half of the nineteenth century and when the Liberals stood for Home Rule all round, but even in the 1960s and 1970s when Plaid Cymru made quite modest electoral gains. Until this decade the instinctive response of English Conservative leaders even to minor troubles (by world standards) was disproportionate pre-emptory conciliation (Welsh television, the equality of the language in the courts, signs and placenames etc. – whether the majority of non-Welsh-speaking Welsh wanted these things or not), not an almost hysterical incantation that 'the sovereignty of Parliament' is threatened – the kind of reaction that (thinking of 1688) George Savile, the Marquis of Halifax, nicknamed 'the Trimmer', once called 'true heart of oak ignorance' or 'stout resolute nonsense'.

The extent of variation in national institutions makes the textbook picture of the United Kingdom as an homogenous society misleading, itself more part of the Whig eighteenth-century ideology than a true description of the politics and societies of the United Kingdom. But as the regulatory machinery of government grew in the late nineteenth century and accelerated as a consequence of the two World Wars and welfare legislation, no attempt was made to devolve power. The relative powers of the regions to the centre declined still more. The legal powers of parliamentary sovereignty could be used against the component parts of the Union, and were used drastically in the prorogation of the Stormont Parliament in 1972; but ordinarily they were not used. Most of the new centralism came about by default, but now it is being added to by intention. Yet history cannot be wholly rewritten or ignored. The United Kingdom is of such a nature that heavy-handed rationalising programmes from the centre can threaten its unity. Historically the United Kingdom after 1707 might be better described as quasi-federal in relation to its actual administration and to what is always extremely important, the sense of identity of its peoples: always a dual identity, Scottish and British, Welsh and British, Ulster Protestant and (whether the rest of us like it or not) British, English and British. But it is the majority English who today seem to be losing this appreciative or tactful sense of dual identity, and are revealing, perhaps for the first time, a dangerous lack of a sense of history.

We live with a dangerous conceptual confusion, especially those who believe in firm principles but not in thought. We confuse legal theory with political theory. 'Parliamentary sovereignty' does indeed mean that only Parliament can make or authorise binding laws, but it does not mean that Parliament cannot delegate and disperse power as political prudence would suggest it should. The distinction between theory and practice was deliberately blurred, as the quotation from Blackstone showed, as part of Whig ideology trying to hold together the United Kingdom in the days of Irish and Scottish rebellions and unrest. But have we not by 1988 outgrown the urgent needs of 1688? 'If sovereignty is questioned, things fall apart', was the old message. But empirically the contrary can often be equally true: 'If sovereignty is exercised arbitrarily and unwisely, things fall apart.' We lost the first British Empire because Lord North, though no philosopher, believed that there was a metaphysical entity called 'sovereignty' which could never be divided – so peace proposals in 1775 and 1776 were rejected out of hand. The chance to conciliate Ireland was lost with Conservative opposition to Home Rule both in 1886 and in 1911–14. No peace can be made with the Argentine, to the peril of their new and fragile democracy because 'sovereignty is not negotiable' (the thoughts of a non-thinker). No lasting solution of the Northern Ireland problem is possible, either, while two governments both take that same high muddled view of sovereignty. Our rulers have ended up by believing their own rhetoric – the confusion of the legal power to legislate with the political prudence to devolve, sometimes indeed to renounce, that legal right. The concept has become not the key to British constitutional thought but the rust in the lock.

DECENTRALISATION AND CITIZENSHIP

In the 1970s one common argument for English regional devolution and for Scottish and Welsh Assemblies was to prevent overload in the centre: that not merely Whitehall but London and the South-East had grown too great. This is a real and still growing problem. Dispersal of some government offices to the provinces is quite irrelevant. The problem lies in the over-concentration of decision-making, publishing and communications, in one very powerful but myopic part of the United Kingdom – London and the Home Counties. It is almost as if the capital, in the eyes of most opinion-makers, because they live there to make their careers, has become the whole country. And this over-concentration both of economic resources and of cultural dominance ('hegemony'?) will continue, until a genuine and self-sustaining dispersal of decision-making to elected bodies helps revivify or create provincial or national centres of power.

Consider even our recent past. Consider Birmingham and Manchester as great cities and as both schools and arenas of citizenship and recruitment grounds for national leadership.[7] Their civic leaders, as of Edinburgh, Glasgow, Liverpool, Sheffield, Leeds, Newcastle, Swansea, Cardiff, Bristol were frequently national figures, exercising real power, not merely in local administration but in the councils of their national parties. When they came to Parliament, or sent colleagues to Parliament, these men knew their local world, a different England, even just to consider England alone for a moment, than London and the Home Counties. One of the continual themes of the English novel from the time of George Eliot and Arnold Bennett, through D. H. Lawrence even into C. P. Snow, has been 'roots', the pull between the provincial culture and the wider world; but it was always a balance of gain and loss, sometimes of disillusionment and homecoming. Most self-made politicians of the older generation lived in two worlds. They made their name on a local stage before a national. The number who found seats any old where after making a national name in London have always been much exaggerated. Indeed the older type of Conservative MP lived in two worlds too, town and country, more often in the other order of emphasis. And both the industrialists and trade unionists were physically and psychologically close to their workplaces. But the newly-dominant world of finance capital in the City of London creates no roots and few loyalties of any kind.

Plainly citizenship needs more to thrive on than spasmodic public elections. It needs an active concern with local as well as national issues; and levels, concern and participation are very much a function of whether there are important decisions to be made and of uncertainty about their outcome. The way to revive inner cities is not to take away the powers of city governments; on the contrary, it is to give them more. The very number and calibre of people wanting to enter into local politics diminishes with the declining discretion allowed to local government and its overburdening with routine tasks dictated by the centre, both so dramatically accelerated by the deliberate policy of Mrs Thatcher's governments. To have to administer the gathering of the unwanted poll tax is the crowning insult to local democracy.

Only MPs themselves and party activists now approximate to the ideal of active citizens rather than passive and spasmodically grateful (or not) good subjects. And MPs themselves are now a fairly cowed if loyally noisy lot. The old informal restraints on governments unchecked by constitutional law, very much depended on the political and constitutional beliefs, the ethics and code, of their own backbenchers. But the old Tory tradition of independence among private members has virtually gone, with a few bold exceptions. The inter-party opposition are now nearly all discarded Ministers, generals with the odd loyal bodyservant but with no regular troops; so the Grandees can be discounted politically. Backbenchers are office-hungry and the only offices that now satisfy them are in Whitehall; the Town Hall is no longer an alternative. With their eggs in one basket, they walk very carefully. And recruitment has changed. The time needed for local government service make firms increasingly reluctant to see their bright juniors stand for office, and there seem few advantages any longer to be got if they do. The most able Conservatives now look to business as a career, not to the House. Prominence in local government now offers few rewards for the ambitious, even those of esteem in the national party. In the House itself it is get on or get lost.

It is no verbal punning to link citizenship with the civic. The connection lies at the very heart of our whole western tradition of politics. As Labour and Liberal go on about the need to increase the participation of ordinary people in decision-making, in workplace, neighbourhood and so on, and denounce the narrowness of the base of existing participation in decision-making, even this inadequate base, necessary to preserve if only to build upon, is being swiftly eroded. Despite their rhetoric, most politicians feel their constituencies more and more an encumbrance to their main career in Parliament, and feel too helpless in the face of national trends even to have much political effect on their own manor. This could, of course, all change utterly if local authorities and regions were given greater powers, including revenue-raising powers.

Conservatives who care about local government (and they usually control a majority of local councils) have themselves to blame, not just their obsessive leader. Unlike Labour and Liberal radicals, they have always been a little ambivalent or nervous about encouraging real citizenship. They have habitually preferred the image of the law-abiding, not law-changing, *good subject.* Historically they had to adjust rapidly to the new world of a democratic franchise (the legacy of Disraeli with the shrewd advice of Walter Bagehot). They stirred themselves and strutted around the country more, but they played the card, as Bagehot foresaw, of *noblesse oblige* in the confident expectation of widespread deference. How unsuited they were in the old days to politics in the colonies – the Irish and the Scots throve better. There was an envy of 'the gentleman' but it all came to dislike and distrust. This great cultural image played a large role in British politics, and education. Its positive side was a code of decent conduct, a certain (if limited) tolerance and a paternalistic care for 'their people'. It also acted as a restraint on their leaders, a restraint both self-imposed (as in Baldwin) and imposed by the party (as finally against Chamberlain). But this code is plainly in decline, whether because there are fewer gentlemen now (rather than, say, careerists), or fewer people who pay any attention to them. But this is, nonetheless, another informal restraint gone. Perhaps the idea that constitutional conventions were a sufficient restraint without formal constitutional law was itself part of this gentleman culture, so knowledgeable about personal codes of conduct, so distrustful of formal laws and intellect, so masculine, indeed male-dominated, in its enjoyment of parliamentary politics as mock combat or a kind of bloodless bloodsport. Yet the popularisation of this cultural image, often blamed for the gentrification of the Victorian 'industrial spirit', is less often blamed for the frustration in Britain of the idea and practice of citizenship. Citizenship is far more evident in France, Holland, the United States, Sweden, Switzerland and the postwar Federal Republic of Germany (a proof that conscious change is possible).

An interesting example of Conservative ambivalence about citizenship is their attitude to political education in local authority schools. Ten years ago many Conservative leaders were not against it, as such – even if they tended to think instinctively that the real object was somehow to instil 'respect for the rule of law' rather than balanced appraisal of real political issues. I remember accompanying Kenneth Baker Mark I to wait on the then Secretary of State for Education, Shirley Williams, to press the case for urging more political education in schools. He pushed warmly on what then seemed an open door.[8] But ten years later Kenneth Baker Mark II produces a national curriculum (a bad enough piece of authoritarian centralism in itself) with no place in it whatever for civic education. This is partly the new intolerance, partly a crudely utilitarian view of the training (hardly education) needed for other people's children, and partly because political education is the very kind of activity that makes the new breed distrust local government as such. Some LEAs do, indeed, think it their duty to try to produce citizens. Local government itself is a school of citizenship. But officially all that is now wanted are skilled workers, occasional voters and regular taxpayers. The great republican image of men and women as citizens has collapsed into a philistine and utilitarian slum. They talk of 'higher standards' but they offer 'prolefeed'.

Decentralisation as part of constitutional reform is all the more needed because of the great Thatcherite paradoxes, so often noted: that when the central state insists on dealing directly with individuals, local institutions have to be rendered either powerless or unattractive; and when the state in the name of liberty seeks to control local initiatives of government, it has to strengthen its own powers to a quite illiberal extent. So many Conservative councillors must now feel that their own feet have been shot off to remove a rotten toe-nail on someone else. It is, of course, not normal politics: it is obsession, and what our ancestors called arbitrary government. We need institutions and laws to contain the obsessive, even ourselves against our own obsessions.

CONCEPTUAL REFORM

There is another way of looking at the whole problem of power. De Tocqueville once reproved John Stuart Mill for linking liberty solely to the rights of individuals; he offered the opinion that there must be a sociological as well as a legal and philosophical condition of liberty: a plurality of intermediary groups between the individual and the state. De Tocqueville admitted that many such groups enshrined privileges and vested interests, and however much reformed by public law some inequities and anomalies would remain; but that would be better for liberty than attempts by the state to deal directly and only with individuals by means of general legislation. That was more likely to lead to what he called (with Napoleonic plebiscites in mind) 'elective despotism'. Mill, being a reasonable and open-minded fellow, compared to Thatcher, Tebbit and Baker, was persuaded. His future writings stressed the need to nourish communities and to extend, while reforming, local government, not simply to sweep it away.

Among socialists there was a debate similar to that between the two greatest liberal thinkers, though more public and less amicable – that between Marx and Proudhon. Proudhon at that time had a larger following than Marx and was to have a lasting influence too, though one still underestimated. He was not an anarchist, as Marx accused him and as anarchists were to claim: he believed in a minimal state, rather like some modern neo-liberals, with largely administrative and coordinatory functions, but alongside the state there should be the most active network of self-governing cooperative communities. His vision was idealistic in sweep and fanciful in detail; but underlying it there was the good sense that power, if both sovereign and centralised, is inherently despotic, and that democratic power can be active and powerful but should be dispersed in 'communities'. Ideally communities would be small enough for everyone to know everyone else, or in practice at least to know the community intimately – like a neighbourhood in its literal sense. And these communities would then group themselves into federations.[9]

Harold Laski went so far as to argue that all power is inherently federal, using that term in a broad sense where many would say 'pluralistic'.[10] He argued, following the Anglo-Catholic Figgis on modern church–state relations and the French socialist Deguit on trade unions, that the theory that the state is sovereign only has relevance to periods of state-formation and of nation-building, and to times of real national emergency. Here he differed from the syndicalists to whom the state was simply a group among other groups and only productive groups were important. No power is in fact absolute, and attempts to enforce claims to a monopoly of decision-making are both oppressive and, in the long run, destabilising. He thought that both the Fabians and the Leninists had made the same mistake as Thomas Hobbes: confusing sovereignty as a minimal necessary condition for political order with a full and sufficient account of the normally highly political mode of operation of states dealing with, indeed partly composed of, a multitude of interest groups.

To Laski local government was not simply an historical relic or a limited grant of powers by the central state subject to good behaviour; it was part of a seamless web of power, stretching up and down. It was the primary manifestation of popular power. Local communities seek to preserve themselves whether their formal powers are tightly proscribed or residual; and many 'sovereign states' are, in fact, either in pitiful vassalage to greater states, or preserve their internal autonomy with constant difficulty, compromises and tradeoffs. This he regarded as a realistic analysis of what actually happens in the governing of states, and he relegated the doctrine of sovereignty to the melodrama of preserving the state in crisis (and warned against the deliberate creation of crises to justify the production of melodramas). The ordinary life of states is the continual necessity of balancing or conciliating group interests, economic and geographical, religious and sometimes ethnic: the image of applying central sovereign power to obtain clear solutions is a misleading, even dangerous, picture of political life.

WHAT FORM OF INSTITUTIONAL REFORM?

I may have seemed to be taking a long time reaching a practical point. But reform can only follow from looking at the problem in its most basic and simplest perspective. The detail is fortuitous and variable: the starting point is crucial. Part of the problem are centralist attempts to legislate detailed good for others; and part is a mistaken formulation of the nature of the British constitution. The solution lies not simply in emancipating ourselves mentally from the old Whig sovereignty ideology, sovereignty invoked to help hold the new, precariously united kingdom together, but in (i) appreciating that we are a union and not a monolithic nation state; and (ii) in comprehending the need to disperse power and to avoid uniform rules if liberty is to be secure and if a diversity of popular demands are to be met. Most popular demands are best realised locally and therefore the results can never be equal, even if arguably they are equitable if people want such differences. My comrades in the Labour Party cannot have it both ways.

If the above analysis is correct it follows that there can be no one model of devolution throughout the United Kingdom. Scotland, Wales and Northern Ireland raise different possibilities for constitutional reform than does England.

The case for Scottish home rule is obvious and lies in Scottish history, tradition and clearly expressed Scottish opinion – opinion that overwhelmingly favours a subsidiary parliament within the United Kingdom, not separation. The case against is based on the peculiarly English fear that any such parliament would necessarily lead to separation. This fear has no reality in Scottish opinion or circumstances but is simply an abstract inference from uncritically-held sovereignty theory: an inference that is absurd when applied to stable federal states throughout the world. Scotland is a nation but only extreme nationalists (and their extreme opponents) argue that for every nation there must be a separate sovereign state. But nations must have some national, representative and expressive institution.

Debate about powers and composition can be endless. But it is obvious that whatever is done must be sufficient to be acceptable and also capable of evolution. For all its faults, the 1978 Act is still the most likely starting-point for a new departure, if revenue-raising provisions are added to it, as the Scottish Labour Party now argues. The late John Mackintosh was vehement in his attacks on the imperfections of the 1978 Bill, but he argued that it was better to set something to work that could be changed after experience rather than wait for ideal agreement.[11]

Far better, however, to proceed through a constitutional convention in which an elected convention would produce a Bill to bring to Parliament – even if that Bill was simply a reform of the 1978 one. Parliament would be wise, in the election of that convention, as in subsequent elections for a Scottish Parliament, to insist, as for the abortive Northern Ireland Convention of 1975–76, the Northern Ireland Assembly elections in the 1980s and the Northern Ireland seats in the European Parliament, on proportional representation. The Labour Party in Scotland should think again on this if they really wish to be seen as generous, patriotic and prudent leaders of a national movement, rather than simply as partisan inheritors and exploiters of it. Consensus is not needed for policy decisions but it is needed for setting up procedural rules, especially a set so elaborate as for a subsidiary parliament; and also because in Scotland local government reform, both in the sense of areas and powers, is quite inseparable from constitutional reform. With a Scottish parliament, the size of the Strathclyde Region becomes unnecessary, indeed in the short run is an interest – as everyone admits privately – against reform.

In Wales the case for proceeding by a constitutional convention rather than directly by a Bill in Parliament is even stronger. The old Act was so overwhelmingly rejected in the referendum because there was no clear agreement by a majority what form any devolution should take to be acceptable and workable.[12] The language question is still an obstacle for most, even if an end in itself for some. Separation is no longer an issue. The Welsh Language Society are now well aware that if the language were not protected by Westminster it could be diminished in a genuine assembly for all Wales. And it is hard to think of further concessions to the Welsh-speaking minority that would bring Plaid Cymru into any Assembly that did not give equal status to the two languages in the Assembly. But this would be a stumbling-block to the Labour Party in Wales, and probably to the Liberals too. Simultaneous translation could, of course, be available on the floor as in the European Parliament and the Dail Eirean (where, in fact, Irish is rarely spoken). Polyglot documentation is only a technical problem. But this would mean that all the staff would have to be fully bilingual, which would mean, in fact, overwhelming sympathy with either Plaid or the Welsh Language Society. And that would be politically unacceptable to the majority of non-Welsh-speaking Welsh members. Or could Plaid cease to be a political party running candidates and simply become a national movement? Since I am not arguing, like some old Liberals, for an imposed uniform solution of devolution for the whole of Great Britain, it is enough to say that Parliament should be very tolerant of any agreement that looked half-way workable that would come from a Constitutional Convention for Wales – whether for a legislative assembly for the Principality, a consultative council or simply more powers for local government.

In Northern Ireland the immediate lines of constitutional policy are already clear and agreed between the British and Irish governments: the recreation of some kind of power-sharing or inter-community assembly in Northern Ireland, and the continuance of the Inter-Governmental Council. That Council, itself an interesting innovation (we can innovate when we have to), retains all law enforcement and formal sovereignty in British hands; but it gives the Irish Government the right to be consulted over any aspect of the government of Northern Ireland. And it reaffirms what is already in two statutes: that Northern Ireland is a part of the United Kingdom, until such time as a majority in a legally constituted poll vote otherwise. The British Government actually pledged itself as part of the 1986 Agreement to bring in legislation for separation should that day come. Northern Ireland is not then, as Unionists would wish, an integral and unconditional part of the United Kingdom like Yorkshire: it is a conditional part. 'The Guarantee' is a two-edged blade. Legal sovereignty can, after all, be a marvellously flexible thing when it is viewed politically and not ideologically.[13]

Our critique of the theory of sovereignty suggests, however, that any acceptable solution is unlikely while the question is put in the form of whether Northern Ireland be part of the Republic of Ireland, with guarantees to the new minority (and some form of weak external link to the United Kingdom), or remain part of the United Kingdom, with even stronger guarantees to the present minority (with some form of weak external link to the Republic)? And still less likely when put in the form, 'whose cause is just?' or that bloodstained ecumenical slogan, 'God Defend the Right!' The facts of the case suggest that Northern Ireland could no more be governed peaceably from Dublin than it can be directly from London. In fact, of course, what is called 'direct rule' is not integration but overall British control of the policies of a Northern Ireland administration, itself as different from Whitehall in personnel and practices and as geographically removed as the Scottish Office.

The logic of the situation is that Northern Ireland inherently faces both ways. And the cussed two-headedness is not just that some of its inhabitants want to be Irish and some British, but that each individual also contains a different mixture of both, culturally and politically. The truth of this, so unwelcome to the zealots in both communities, is seen in the suspicion of Northerners in the South and in the maddening lack of reciprocity in England to the loyalism of the Loyalists. The logic of the situation, as already immanent in the Inter-Governmental Council, points towards some kind of joint responsibility for the level of decisions that would normally be taken by a central government in a formal federation, while an assembly in Northern Ireland handles at least the kind of powers of a normal federal province. The concept that is now common is 'joint authority', of course, tactfully not 'joint sovereignty'. Already, in fact, with referenda, constitutional conventions and electoral reform, the British Constitution has proved, in response to unusual problems, more flexible and inventive than as yet Conservative and Labour leaders will allow is possible on the mainland.

The main alternatives for a structure of regional government in England were set out briefly but clearly in the White Paper of July 1974, *Devolution Within the United Kingdom: Some Alternatives for Discussion* and *Devolution: the English Dimension: a consultative document* of December 1976. Because of the defeat of devolution in the referenda and the subsequent fall of the Labour Government, politicians have for the moment forgotten them. But they are likely to be the starting-point of new initiatives. Neither put forward a precise scheme; the political will was not there. But the 1976 document ended with what could be the broad outline of the future:

> 88. To sum up, the case for change is seen to lie in:
> (a) lightening the burden on central government, enabling it to concentrate on matters of genuinely national importance;
> (b) bringing government closer to the people;
> (c) rendering the work of major nominated bodies subject to local democratic control; and
> (d) providing a layer of government to deal with such matters as may better be dealt with at a level intermediate between central and local government as they now exist.

The whole document hardly, in the words of the Greek anthology, 'warms the blood like wine': and I would move the deletion of the last four words. But even then the case was clear for a powerful intermediary level of regional or provincial government, just as now it is clear that local government needs restoring and strengthening. A lot of economic and geographical thinking went into establishing the boundaries of the seven Planning Regions of 1965. What was lacking was any elective basis for the boards and a broad political perspective, rather than already-outmoded ideas of economic planning and development.[14]

New regions would need to be seen as having capital cities, existing centres whose decline as informal provincial capitals, like Bristol, Birmingham, Leeds, Manchester and Nottingham, can be reversed. If we are to disperse power, both on the provincial or regional and on the local level, one must build on the culture and civic ambiance of cities. This would argue for the old eight 'New Standard Regions' of 1961, especially as their more traditional criteria would separate East Anglia from London and the South East, included for economic reasons in 1965, bringing Norwich into play as a provincial capital. In 1964 it seemed rational to *accept* the growing dominance of East Anglia by the London region; but part of the object of a new constitutional settlement should be to contain the power and excessive prestige of the one city-region which is also the national capital. 'The city-region' is the only viable political and economic concept. The power of London and the attraction of it to people of ability cumulates not just because of a centralised administration but because of the facilities of the city and its region. The rebuilding of city centres elsewhere already gives something to build on. Capitals must look like capitals if power is to be federalised.

I argue that power should be federalised, not that we necessarily need a formal federal system. We need a Bill of Rights. We need electoral reform. We need a new structure of government for Scotland, Wales and Northern Ireland, and we need directly elected English provinces with revenue-raising options as well as guaranteed central funding by agreed formulas. But the attitude of mind comes first. It is more important to change some of our presuppositions about 'parliamentary sovereignty' and the nature of power than to state an intricate case for a probably impossible written constitution of the United Kingdom with entrenched constitutional law and an American-style Supreme Court. We would need a legal profession on the American model before we would be likely to trust lawyers with such power, and perhaps not even then. Both the democratic and the oligarchic spirit work against it. We will probably proceed on the Stormont model.

That name is not enticing nor is the memory of the folly of its unchecked majorities, but the thought is serious. The difficulties of Parliament legislating to bind its successors irrevocably in law are immense. Sovereignty theory in the tradition of this country does, I have noted, have a strong point on jurisdictions. Like the Act of Union, fundamental reforms could be gone back upon in theory; but because of the political difficulties and the popular support surrounding them, they would only be reversed in extreme circumstances: like the abolition of the Stormont Parliament. Parliament will retrain its legal sovereignty. It would create provincial assemblies by ordinary statute as it might create, for tightly-defined purposes, a constitutional jurisdiction. Such acts when passed would be politically difficult to amend, not legally so. The whole difficulty will be in ever getting them passed. Parliament would be overwhelmingly wise to devolve much power: for the sake of liberty, to avoid overload, to reanimate civic spirit and to maintain the fundamental nature of the United Kingdom as a quasi-federation. And it should legislate more and more in the form of enabling acts and delegated legislation, not for Ministers to complete, but to allow wide discretion to all subsidiary assemblies and councils. The remit to the 1919 Speaker's Conference used a phrase quite shocking and contradictory both to strict sovereignty theorists and to strict legal federalists: 'federal devolution'. But it was a sensible phrase. I like to think of myself now as a political federalist.

Constitutional reform and the devolution of powers will not, of course, come by reason, any more than the Reform Bills came by reason. It is only likely to come either when a government is frightened of the political consequence of not reforming or when a government cannot be sure of a regular majority in the Commons, and in any case not until the fall of Thatcher. But if that day comes, then I think it will all come quickly and come together, not piece by piece. We should, in memory of 1688, if we have any care for national constitutional celebration and continued reputation, prepare our thoughts so that we can get it right when the opportunity comes; as men in exile did before that fortunate year.

Notes

1. Sir Ivor Jennings, *The Law and the Constitution*, Allen & Unwin, London, 1948, and see also Geoffrey Marshal and Graeme Moodie, *Some Problems of the Constitution*, Hutchinson, London, 1964.
2. J. C. Banks, *Federal Britain*, Harrap, London, 1971, pp. 81–5 – an unusually thoughtful and surprisingly neglected book.
3. Quoted in Vernon Bogdanor, *Devolution*, Oxford University Press, Oxford, 1979, p. 163. The merits of his analysis of the problems of Northern Ireland, Scotland and Wales should *not* have been affected by the fact the book was published before the referenda on the assumption that they would pass.
4. See for example, *Power to the Provinces*, Liberal Party, London, 1968, and J. C. Banks, *Federal Britain*, op. cit., pp. 79–95, which reports a continuous drip and trickle of Liberal Private Members' motions and 'ten-minute' Bills from the 1930s through to the 1970s.
5. Antony Wright, 'The Politics of Constitutional Reform', *Political*

Quarterly, October 1986, pp. 414–25. The article concentrates on the Bill of Rights. Wright sees its connection with electoral reform, but is silent (like many other Fabian writers still) on devolution. Richard Rose's remarkable *Understanding the United Kingdom: the territorial dimension in government*, Longman, London, 1982, is the pioneering modern textbook of the totality, not Anglo-centric in the least; but conceptually it is weak on 'state', 'sovereignty' and 'power' and ends unexpectedly as an Ulster and a Scottish Unionist tract.

6. These next paragraphs draw on my 'The Sovereignty of Parliament and the Irish Question' in Desmond Rea (ed.), *Political Cooperation in Divided Societies*, Macmillan, Dublin, 1982, pp. 229–54. On the general question of 'sovereignty' and United Kingdom politics, the first chapter of H. V. Heuston, *Essays in Constitutional Law*, Second edition, Stevens, London, 1964, is profound and stimulating.
7. M. J. Wiener, *English Culture and the Decline of the Industrial Spirit*, Cambridge University Press, Cambridge, 1981, is magisterial, though he underestimates the purely political culture; see Antony Wright, 'British Decline: Economic or Political?', *Parliamentary Affairs*, January 1987, pp. 41–56 for a good survey of this whole controversy.
8. Following the Report of a working party of the Hansard Society, published as Bernard Crick and Alex Porter (eds), *Political Education and Political Literacy*, Longman, London, 1978.
9. See my *Socialism*, Open University Press, Milton Keynes, 1987, pp. 39–42. The whole book tries to restore the historical balance between pluralist and *étatist* socialist thought, as does David Blunkett and Bernard Crick, *The Labour Party's Aims and Values: an unofficial statement*, Spokesman Books, Nottingham, 1988.
10. In his early scholarly books on the theory of sovereignty and in his once-famous *A Grammar of Politics*, Allen & Unwin, London, 1928, not in his later Marxist writings.
11. See throughout in the post-humous volume, Henry Drucker (ed.), *John P. Mackintosh on Scotland*, Longman, London, 1982.
12. See David Foulkes, J. Barry Jones, R. A. Wilford (eds), *The Welsh Veto: the Wales Act 1978 and the Referendum*, University of Wales Press, Cardiff, 1983.
13. As more fully argued in my 'Northern Ireland and the Concept of Consent' in Carol Harlow (ed.), *Public Law and Politics*, Sweet & Maxwell, London, 1986. See also W. Harvey Cox, 'Managing Northern Ireland Intergovernmentally: an appraisal of the Anglo-Irish Agreement', *Parliamentary Affairs*, January 1987, pp. 80–97; he concludes that while the Agreement was 'a fine and imaginative political enterprise', yet the two governments 'were themselves too much in the thrall of their own inheritance of simplistic concepts of sovereignty and territoriality, which ill fitted the peculiarity of Northern Ireland' (p. 97).
14. An excellent summary of the whole local government reform controversy is found in W. A. Hampton, *Local Government and Politics*, Longman, London, 1986, pp. 164–82.

5 Britain and Europe: the Myth of Sovereignty[1]

Vernon Bogdanor

'Now that you are a fact, we shall deal with you.'

Sir Roger Makins to Jean Monnet, 1952,
after the formation of the European Coal and Steel Community
without British participation.[2]

I

On the Continent, by contrast with Britain, constitutional arrangements are taken seriously. The six countries which originally formed the European Community – France, West Germany, Italy and the Benelux countries – had all suffered either the collapse of democratic institutions under the impact of Fascism or the indignity of military defeat and occupation. For them, constitutional arrangements were not a distraction from the real substance of politics, but a precondition for the return of a stable democratic order.

The British approach to constitutional issues, on the other hand, is permeated by a belief that they are an unnecessary distraction from the real agenda of politics, which is socioeconomic. This is perhaps understandable in the light of our uniquely fortunate history. Whereas the West German state began its existence in 1949, and the French state was reconstituted in 1946 and renewed in 1958, there is no date at which Britain can be said to have *begun* as a constitutional entity. We have often felt the need to make adjustments to our institutions, but not – since the seventeenth century at least – to recreate the state. This affects, in a very profound way, our attitude towards the European Community. Indeed, on the central issue of what kind of entity the European Community should become, Britain's perception is quite different from that of the founding countries.

When we joined the Community in 1973, we entered what British governments, both Conservative and Labour, saw as a commercial arrangement, an organisation dedicated to the removal of trade barriers, not a dynamic entity whose purpose was to 'unify Europe'. Indeed, European Union is a concept which most British politicians profess not to understand. In November 1984, Mrs Thatcher declared that she 'would like to know what is meant by it before I could tell whether I was for it or against it'.

Thus, throughout the period in which reform of the European Community – designed to make it both more democratic and more effective – has been under discussion, Britain's attitude has been one of which De Gaulle might have been proud: negative, insular and hostile to any encroachment upon national sovereignty. Only if Britain's veto is preserved, successive governments have argued, can British interests be properly defended. So it is that Britain regularly finds herself lining up, on institutional questions, with the sceptical Danes, and with Andreas Papandreou's Greece, in the camp of those opposed to the further development of the European Community.

That it is in Britain's interests to ape De Gaulle is generally taken for granted as being something beyond dispute. The purpose of what follows, however, is to argue that this position is entirely counterproductive, not only from the point of view of the progress of the Community but from the standpoint of Britain's national interests. The notion of British sovereignty is not only an anachronism in an era of multinational enterprise and technology; it serves also to blind British governments to the true interests of those whom they represent. To see why this is so, it is necessary to look at the problems facing the European Community, and consider how it might best overcome them.

II

At the outset, two conflicting perceptions are bound to strike any observer of Community affairs. The one is of a Community making enthusiastic progress towards the completion of a single internal market. The other is of a Community in recurrent crisis, facing continual difficulties in resolving its budgetary or agricultural problems and repeatedly on the verge of financial collapse. There is a sense in which both perceptions are true.

There can be no doubt of the enthusiasm with which Community officials and heads of government – including Britain – look forward to the completion of the internal market scheduled for 1992. By that date, all non-tariff barriers to trade and many tiresome frontier controls which add considerably to the cost of finished goods, should have been abolished, and there should be a single domestic market for goods and services throughout the Community.

How is it, then, that each meeting of the European Council – the forum for regular summits of Community heads of state and government – is accompanied by lurid headlines in the popular press asking whether the Community is bankrupt and whether it can ever recover? Why is it that the Community seems unable to resolve its budgetary problems or reform what is widely regarded as a ruinously extravagant Common Agricultural Policy? How is one to reconcile two such opposed perceptions?

The central problem facing the European Community is that it is – potentially at least – an economic giant while remaining a political dwarf. Community leaders while pursuing economic and social goals of vital importance to the future of their countries have given insufficient attention to the constitutional changes which would enable the Community to underpin its economic strength.

The difficulties facing the Community in its attempts to control its budget and reform its Common Agricultural Policy, signify not a breakdown of the Community, but of the methods by which it has been governed, especially since the establishment of the European Council in 1974. The Council, so it was held, could provide the Community with the leadership it so badly needed during a period of economic turmoil and international insecurity. Yet recent summits have shown how inadequate this conception of the government of the Community really is. Can a Europe of 330 million people, an entity larger than the United States or the Soviet Union, really be governed by twelve political leaders meeting twice a year for 24–30 hours and seeking to reach unanimous agreement on the major problems besetting the Community? 'We have got to get agreement among all of them', Mrs Thatcher told the House of Commons on 8 December 1987, explaining why the Copenhagen Summit had caused such ructions. 'Each is naturally concerned to do the best for his own country. It is not easy.' The same point was put rather more grandiloquently by President Mitterrand of France in his speech before the European Parliament on 24 May 1984: 'How can a complex and diversified unit that the Community has become be governed by the rules of the Diet of the old kingdom of Poland, where every member could block decisions? We all know where that led . . .'

The methods by which the Community is currently governed fail in two interconnected ways. First, they are inefficient. They do not lead to rapid or effective decision-making. Second, they do not meet those standards of democratic accountability which member states are accustomed to expect in their own domestic affairs. These deficiencies are interconnected since the Community is unlikely to become more effective unless it also becomes more democratic. Indeed, the more successful the Community proves to be in the implementation of common policies, and, in particular, the more rapidly it is able to complete the single internal market, the more insistent will be the complaints about the lack of proper accountability. If the Community is to become an effective economic entity, member states will have to agree to take more decisions on a Community basis. If, for example, a European Monetary Fund were to be created, there would be the nucleus of a European central bank. There has so far been too little discussion on how such a bank could be placed under constitutional control. European institutions are not yet powerful enough to assume the wide economic and social responsibilities which further development of the Community will entail.

Member states, however, cannot be expected to transfer further important powers to the Community without the assurance that the Community is being governed effectively and that its decision-making procedures are efficient. And, equally important, neither electors nor the national parliaments which represent their interests, *ought* to be asked to surrender powers at present under their own control to a supranational authority not subject to proper democratic accountability. Thus, if the Community is to be able to carry out its new tasks effectively, its institutions need greater authority and a more democratic structure.

III

The central deficiency in the operation of Community institutions is that those institutions which represent the supranational element in the Community – the Commission and the European Parliament – find themselves in a much weaker position than the Council of Ministers and the European Council which represent the intergovernmental element of the Community. Because the Council of Ministers has come to be the prime decision-making body on Community policy, policymaking has come to be based more upon inter-governmental agreement than upon the pursuit of common aims. Nor is it at all easy to make the Council of Ministers properly accountable to the electorate of the member states. In theory, of course, the stance of national ministers in the Council of Ministers can be determined by national parliaments, but in practice – except perhaps in Denmark – there is little control or accountability. Indeed, if the other eleven national parliaments were to insist upon the tight degree of control exercised by the Danish Folketing, it is highly doubtful whether the Council of Ministers could *ever* reach decisions which reflected more than the lowest common denominator of agreement.

The Commission, which in the eyes of the Community's founding fathers was intended to act as the main initiator of policy and the executive of the Community, the prime exponent and defender of the Community interest, has found its influence considerably circumscribed. Roy Jenkins, a former President of the Commission, has summed up the role of the President in the following way;

> There are certain fields in which one exercises power, but from the point of view of the direct exercise of power I have less as President of the Commission than I had as a senior British Cabinet Minister . . . basically it is the case that the Commission proposes but the Council – be it the Council of Ministers or the European Council – disposes, and they don't always dispose exactly how we would like them to – particularly when we're trying to move something forward – particularly when we're trying to get something new going.[3]

A main reason for the Commission's lack of power is that it has no parliamentary or popular base. The Council of Ministers represents the governments of the member states, and the European Parliament represents their electorates. Members of the Commission, however, are not fully responsible to the European Parliament, neither are they appointed by the Parliament, nor directly elected. This makes it difficult for the Commission to command the legitimacy necessary to fulfil the initiatory role which the founders of the Community intended it to have.

The European Parliament was conceived as a consultative assembly rather than a fully-fledged legislature. Article 137 of the Treaty of Rome provides for it to exercise 'advisory and supervisory powers' only. It has little direct legislative power except within the budgetary field, and, although it can exert influence, it has only limited control over the Council of Ministers or the European Council. Parliament's weakness has become more pronounced with the emergence of the Council of Ministers and the European Council as the main decision-making bodies of the Community. For, as David Marquand has argued,[4] Parliament's powers, minimal as they are, are wrongly focused, being directed at the Commission which ought, in theory, to be its ally in pressing for common action at European level, rather than at the Council of Ministers, the real decision-making centre of the Community.

Direct elections to the European Parliament have painfully exposed the contrast between the Parliament's popular and democratic base and its comparative lack of power. There cannot be any other Parliament in the democratic world, which is elected by universal suffrage, and yet has so little control over its 'government'. Perhaps it is for this reason that turnout in the European elections has been so disappointing. In 1979, it averaged only 60.7 per cent, and by 1984, this had fallen to 57.0 per cent. And, perhaps even more important, the elections in every member state of the Community were seen, not as transnational European elections, but – like local government elections in Britain – as plebiscites upon the performance of the governments of the member states.

Thus, of the main Community institutions, the Commission, which ought to provide the Community with leadership, has found itself acting too often as the civil service of the Community, while the Council of Ministers and the European Council have come to be its dominant institutions. The European Parliament, although directly elected by universal suffrage, has remained, except on budgetary matters, a primarily consultative assembly, and this has meant that democratic accountability at Community level has been lacking. The consequence is that the Community does not enjoy the political authority of a well-functioning democracy.

Towards the end of his life, in September 1974, Jean Monnet told President Giscard d'Estaing of France, 'I think that what's lacking more than anything in European affairs . . . is authority. Discussion is organised: decision is not. By themselves, the existing Community institutions are not strong enough.'[5]

This, then, is the challenge which the Community faces – how to reform its institutions so that it can carry out effectively and in accordance with the canons of democracy the major economic and social tasks which European governments have laid upon it. How is this challenge to be met?

IV

The Single European Act, adopted by the member states of the Community in 1986, and now ratified by their parliaments, undoubtedly marks a major step forward. The Act provides for two major constitutional changes. First, it extends the range of subjects which can be dealt with by qualified majority voting in the Council of Ministers, rather than, as hitherto, by unanimity. In particular, qualified majority voting is provided for matters connected with Article 100A of the Treaty of Rome, the functioning of the single internal market, defined as 'an area without internal frontiers in which the free movement of goods, persons, services and capital is ensured . . .'

Secondly, the Single European Act gives to the European Parliament a wider role in the legislative process through a new procedure for 'cooperation' between Parliament and the Council of Ministers for the exercise of some European Community powers. Although this provision affects only some ten articles of the Treaty, these include such important areas as the new power for approximating national laws, the powers designed to bring about free movements of workers, and freedom to establish businesses and provide services.

Further, a new Article of the Treaty, Article 149, para. 2(b), opens up the possibility of an entirely new role for the European Parliament. For it requires the Council of Ministers to inform Parliament fully of the *reasons* which lead the Council to adopt a particular common position towards amendments proposed by the European Parliament. This measure has little substantive significance, but it is of some symbolic importance since it offers a first hint that the Council of Ministers has some responsibility to the European Parliament.

V

The Single European Act provides for the first major set of amendments to the Treaty of Rome and other Community Treaties since these treaties came into force, other than those relating to the successive enlargements of the Community and the two budgetary Treaties. What is likely to be the impact of the constitutional changes which it proposes, and how are they likely to affect British interests?

Much of the comment in Britain on the significance of the Act has been fearful in tone – see, for example, the 12th Report of the House of Lords Select Committee on the European Communities: Single European Act and Parliamentary Scrutiny (HL 149: 1985–1986) – complaining of the loss of sovereignty which the Act is likely to entail, and the dangers of surrendering powers to a Community which could possibly develop into that most terrifying of all bodies, a European Federation. In reality, however, the Act is likely to be quite limited in its effects. This is so for a number of reasons.

First, the Act, although it lays down a deadline of 1992 for completion of the internal market, does not make this a matter of legal obligation. It merely reiterates an objective which, according to the Treaty of Rome, should have been completed by 1970! Perhaps it is because it imposes no binding commitment that the Community is already a long way behind the timetable laid down by Lord Cockfield for the 320 measures which need to be passed to achieve a genuine common market. By February 1988, only 70 (under one-half of those required by the timetable) had been passed.

Secondly, although the Single European Act introduces majority voting into an area in which unanimity has hitherto prevailed, unanimity continues to apply on many matters closely related to the internal market, and especially to derogations from the subject-matter of Article 100A, 'fiscal provisions, . . . those relating to the free movements of persons . . . those relating to the rights and interests of employed persons', and it is difficult to see how a real common market can be achieved without common policies in these areas. And one unfortunate consequence of putting European Monetary Union within the Treaty framework is that it becomes subject to a requirement of ratification by all twelve national parliaments. This means that the second phase of European Monetary Union is likely to be more difficult to achieve.

Thirdly, the so-called Luxembourg Compromise – in reality, of course, not a compromise at all, but a convention forced upon the Community by De Gaulle in 1965–6 – remains. The French version of the Compromise which has on the whole prevailed since 1966 is that 'where very important interests are at stake, the discussions must be continued until unanimous agreement is reached'. Yet, in the past, the veto has been used not only to defend 'very important interests' but to defend quite parochial or sectoral interests. In May 1985, for example, Herr Kiechle, the German Agriculture Minister, prevented a farm price agreement because the Commission sought a 0.9 per cent reduction in cereal prices beyond what he was willing to countenance. Around 5 per cent of the population of the Federal Republic is engaged in agriculture, and cereals account for around 10 per cent of total German agricultural production. It would be difficult to argue that the protection of German cereal prices constituted a vital national interest needing to be defended by the veto. But the Luxembourg Compromise has encouraged even member states which wish to see more rapid progress in the Community – such as the Federal Republic – to use their veto on inappropriate issues. The Compromise has in practice become an agreement to disagree, and has meant that member states cannot, in general, be outvoted in the Council of Ministers.

It is a common misconception that, without the Luxembourg Compromise, member states would be forced into accepting policies to which they strongly object. Yet, even without the Compromise, unanimity would still be required for Treaty changes or for additions to the existing Community competencies. Thus, no member state can be compelled to agree to the transfer of new competencies to the Community against its wishes. What the Luxembourg Compromise does is to prevent majority decision-making on the management of *existing* competencies, on competencies which have already been transferred to the Community. In these areas, the unanimity requirement is in effect a decision not to decide, to abide by the status quo. But that too is a decision.

The Luxembourg Compromise has cast a shadow over the whole working of the Community. Its effect has been that where a member state finds itself in a minority, it does not need to argue its case or negotiate with the majority. Each member state is well aware that it cannot be outvoted, and so the search for consensus encourages the lowest common denominator of agreement. Such a procedure is bound to hinder the development of a Community whose whole *raison d'être* is the method of common action.

Yet the Luxembourg Compromise, being a matter of convention rather than law, is not formally affected by the Single European Act. Governments, such as the British, which seek to act as a brake rather than a spur to the Community, profess to believe that the Compromise will operate as it did before. Speaking in the House of Commons on 5 December 1985, Mrs Thatcher claimed that

> the Luxembourg Compromise will still be applied even when there is majority voting, provided that a very important national interest is involved . . . presumably the Luxembourg Compromise will operate as it does now by the declaration of a particular point that is of very important national interest.[6]

But, precisely because the Compromise has no legal force, it has on occasions in the past been possible to implement the provisions of the Treaty if a sufficient majority is prepared to apply these provisions strictly. On one notable occasion, in 1982, Britain tried to use her veto to block a decision on agricultural prices, but the other member states, relying upon the Treaty, insisted upon taking a decision by majority vote.

In fact, the Single European Act is likely to make it more difficult for a member state to invoke the Luxembourg Compromise. This is because the new cooperation procedure provided for by the Act allows the Commission to put forward proposals, which Parliament can amend, and which the Council of Ministers can adopt by a qualified majority; although if the Council wishes to make its own amendments, this can only be done by unanimous vote. With the European Parliament and the Commission in agreement, it becomes more difficult for any single national government to achieve unanimous support to make amendments to Parliament's proposals; and the political momentum which such proposals will have acquired makes it likely that there will be a qualified majority in favour of them in the Council of Ministers, so making the exercise of the veto politically more difficult. It is likely, therefore, that use of the veto will become much less significant in the working of the Community as a result of the passage of the Single European Act. This means that the impact of individual member states on the decisions of the Council of Ministers could diminish considerably, and that they will be outvoted more often. One consequence is that the influence which the Westminster Parliament can bring to bear upon the Europan Community indirectly through its influence on United Kingdom Ministers, will also diminish. Thus, the Single European Act is likely to increase the so-called 'democratic deficit' in the Community, as important areas of policymaking come to be removed from the purview of national parliaments – which is already very limited – without becoming subject to control by the European Parliament.

For the powers of the European Parliament, though extended by the Single European Act, are still primarily negative, powers to reject legislation rather than to secure its implementation. The European Parliament can now block decisions of the Council of Ministers which it does not like; it can veto a package negotiated by others, a veto which can only be overridden by a unanimous vote in the Council of Ministers. What the European Parliament cannot do is to initiate or promote policies against the wishes of the Council of Ministers. It can act as a brake upon European integration, not as an accelerator. But the last word remains with the Council of Ministers. Experience of the new cooperation procedure has so far been very limited. Yet already it seems clear that amendments to European legislation which are not part of the common position of the Council of Ministers (unless they concern only minor detail) have little chance of success.

Despite the increased powers given to the European Parliament by the Single European Act, it is inconceivable that the Community will find itself developing in the near future into a fully-fledged federal state. What is far more probable is that it will advance too slowly – too slowly to offer effective democratic control over the new common policies envisaged by the Single European Act, and too slowly to secure effective cooperation in foreign policy. That was the view of the European Parliament when it accepted the Single European Act only reluctantly, declaring that it 'can produce only modest progress in certain spheres of Community activity, and that it is very far from constituting the genuine reform of the Community that its people need to consolidate their economic position in the world'. (Resolution of the European Parliament, 16 January 1986.)

Unless the structure of the Community can be reformed so as to provide genuine accountability, enthusiasm for the European idea will weaken. The electors of Europe will not support the transfer of national competencies to the Community if that is seen to imply replacing democratic control by national parliaments with non-accountable power. It is for this reason that the constitutional structure of the European Community is so deeply interconnected with its prospects of becoming a genuinely effective protector of the common interests of Europeans.

VI

Can Europe advance rapidly enough to meet the challenge of a new age, an age in which there are tremendous limitations upon the extent to which a single country in an open-market economy can adopt economic policies significantly out of line with the policies of its neighbours, an age in which the progress of arms control makes it likely that there will be a reappraisal of America's budgetary and defence commitments in Europe? The Community will only be able to meet this challenge if it is willing to accept the need for further constitutional change.

As the Community acquires more policy competencies, as it progresses towards the completion of the single internal market, the gap in accountability – the 'democratic deficit' – will become more glaring. If the Community is to become an effective economic entity, then member states will have to agree to take more decisions on a Community basis. But this will only be done if the institutions of the Community are placed under proper democratic control.

This must mean a much greater role for the European Parliament, the only Community institution elected by universal suffrage to represent the interests of Europeans. National parliaments will find themselves unable to make Ministers accountable to them when Community policies impinge even more widely on national policies and when national governments lose the power of veto in the Council of Ministers, so that the Ministers of individual member states will be outvoted more often. The only way in which democratic control can be exercised over the Council of Ministers in such circumstances is for Community decisions to be made subject to the approval of the European Parliament, so giving it a genuine legislative role. Parliament must share legislative power with the Council of Ministers: that is, it must be given the power of co-decision. Jacques Delors, the President of the European Commission, has claimed that co-decision would mean no-decision, that the procedures of the Community would become slower and more cumbersome when the European Parliament and the Council of Ministers were unable to agree. To avoid this possibility, it would be necessary to impose time limits for each phase of the legislative process as is already done with the Community budget, and to some extent, the Single European Act.

VII

The European Parliament, however, can only be strong if it is also representative. But unfortunately Britain remains the only member state not to use proportional representation for elections to the European Parliament, and this has the effect of distorting the composition of the Parliament, and making it less representative than it should be.

The disproportional result in Britain affects the representativeness of the European Parliament by artificially increasing the size of the European Democratic Group, two-thirds of whom are British

Conservatives, at the expense of the Liberal and Democratic Reformist Group, which Alliance MEP's from Britain would probably have joined. It also means that the largest Liberal party in the Community found itself, in 1984, unrepresented in the European Parliament.

In January 1988, the size of the political groups in the European Parliament was as follows:

Socialists	165 seats
European Peoples Party (Christian Democrat)	115 seats
European Democratic Group (Conservative)	66 seats
Communists	48 seats
Liberal and Democratic Reformists	44 seats
European Democratic Alliance	29 seats
Rainbow Group	20 seats
European Right	16 seats
Independents	15 seats

If the election in Britain had been conducted by proportional representation, the Alliance would have won 14 seats instead of none. Thus, the Liberal and Democratic Reformists would have had 58 seats rather than 44. The Conservatives, on the other hand, would have won 33 seats rather than the 45 they actually won. Thus, the European Democratic Group would have had 54 seats rather than 66. The Liberal and Democratic Reformists would then have been the third largest rather than the fifth largest group; while the European Democrats would have been the fourth largest rather than the third.

Thus the failure of Britain to adopt a proportional method of election not only misrepresents the opinion of the British electorate, but upsets the whole balance of the European Parliament, so weakening its authority and legitimacy. The British government should, therefore, assist in fulfilling the requirement in the Treaty of Rome that a uniform electoral procedure be adopted, by accepting the principle of proportional representation for elections to the European Parliament.

VIII

But the Commission, as well as Parliament, needs to be strengthened so that it can once again take up the role, intended for it by the founding fathers of the Community, of being the motor for European integration. This could be done in two different ways. The first would be to make the Commission fully responsible to the European Parliament after the fashion of most parliamentary democracies. This would involve Parliament selecting the Commission and, as now, endorsing it with a vote of confidence before it takes office, and having the power to remove it following a vote of censure passed by a qualified majority. A new Commission would take office after each election to the European Parliament. The Commission would no longer be composed of the nominees of the member states, of varying political affiliations. Instead, it would have a particular political colour – Left or Right as the case may be – depending upon the majority in the European Parliament. This would make the Commission a more cohesive body, better able to provide leadership to the Community. It would also increase the salience, – and possibly therefore the turnout – of elections to the European Parliament, which would become in effect elections to choose a European executive.

The second, and far more radical method of strengthening the Commission, is to elect it directly by universal suffrage in the member states, there being at least one member of the Commission from each member state. For the Community, it might be argued, corresponds less to a parliamentary model of government than to a separation-of-powers model. Making the Commission responsible to the European Parliament would not, on this view, be of much value since it would do nothing to make the Council of Ministers more accountable. Direct election of the Commission, on the other hand, would, by providing the Commission with a powerful popular base, enable it to share power with the Council of Ministers. The Commission and Parliament would represent the electorate of Europe, organised as individuals, while the Council of Ministers would represent the electorate organised through the member states.

The Commission, were it to be directly elected, would have to be elected on a two-ballot system. Each party grouping would nominate its own team of Commissioners comprising one candidate from each member state, headed by a candidate for the Presidency of the Commission. Thus, there might be a Socialist ticket headed by Piet Dankert, a Liberal one headed by Martin Bangemann and a Conservative team headed by Lord Plumb. In addition, there would be Christian Democrat and Communist tickets and no doubt others. The top two tickets from the first ballot would then, as in elections for the French presidency, go forward to contest the second ballot. This would impose upon a European multi-party system, a bipolar organisation of political alternatives – a choice on the second ballot between a broadly Left-leaning ticket and a Rightward one. Thus, direct election of the Commission could serve to clarify choices for the electors of Europe. In addition, it would be likely to have the effect of focusing popular interest on European issues and making them exciting – something that direct elections to the European Parliament have been unable to do. Electors would feel themselves to be genuinely involved in making their own choices for the future of Europe.[7]

IX

The development of the European Community towards European Union is bound to entail the danger of over-centralisation of government as national competencies come to be replaced by Community competencies. That is an inevitable consequence of membership of the Community. If not guarded against, it could alienate electors from government. European Community institutions could appear even more remote than national governments, and the ordinary citizen may feel that he or she has insufficient leverage over decisions taken at Community level. This alienation could endanger the process of European integration.

There are two ways of guarding against it. The first is to adopt the measures outlined above to ensure that the institutions of the Community become more accountable to the electorate. But, however accountable they become, there is still bound to be a transfer of powers from the British Government towards a European layer. Therefore, there must be a second process of counterbalancing this transfer of powers upwards by a transfer of power downwards to the regions and localities of Britain which is already the most centralised state in the Community, the only one of the larger member states without a democratically-elected regional layer of government. This high degree of centralisation, which is already proving irksome, would become intolerable if further powers were removed from Westminster to Brussels. A vital concomitant of the process of closer European integration, therefore, should be a policy of decentralisation and devolution of power so as to ensure that decisions are taken at a level as close to the citizen as possible. The European Community is based upon the premise that the traditional state framework is too small to undertake many of the necessary tasks of modern government. There is no doubt, however, that the state is also too large to carry out many other tasks effectively. With devolution to local government, to a Scottish Parliament, and, in the long run, to Wales and the English regions, British government could become more effective since it would be able to concentrate upon the essential tasks of government without getting bogged down in detailed intervention. Of our Community partners, Belgium, France, Germany, Italy and Spain, have all accepted the logic of this argument. It is time that Britain did so as well.

Thus, devolution and decentralisation, discussed in another chapter in this volume, are complementary to, and not in conflict with European integration. The rationale for both policies is the same – that, in the modern world, the power of government is most effectively exercised when it is shared, rather than emanating only from one focal point. Or, to put the point in a different way, both policies – European integration and devolution – highlight the inadequacies of the Hobbesian and very British conception of sovereignty.

X

Are the above proposals entirely utopian? One should be wary of dismissing them in this way. The modest advances made by the Single European Act would scarcely have been possible without the work of dedicated utopians such as the late Altiero Spinelli, under whose auspices the European Parliament produced the Draft Treaty on European Union which spurred governments to action. All too often in the history of the European Community, it is the utopians of yesterday who turn out to have become the realists of today. And was not the Community itself, and its forerunner the Coal and Steel Community, the product of utopian thinking – and dismissed as such at the time by successive British governments, much to our disadvantage?

Moreover, there is considerable evidence to show that the British government seriously underestimates the potential willingness of the British people to support moves towards greater European integration. Successive *Eurobarometer* surveys, charting the movement of opinion in the member states, have shown, in their analysis of British opinion, what the authors of a recent survey describe as 'an impressive, steady evolution towards clearly "pro-European" positions. They have not yet reached the average of the countries that signed the Treaties in Rome, 30 years ago. But they have totally reversed the basic trend in their public opinion towards the Community. If we compare their answers to the "United States of Europe" question of 17 years ago to their present day replies, a dramatic change comes to the fore. While, in 1970, 30% of the British were in favour of a "United States of Europe", but 48% against, today 52% (that is 58% of those who reply) are in favour and only 37% remain hostile to this idea (i.e. 42% of those who reply)' (*Eurobarometer*, March 1987, p. v). There is in Britain, as in most of the Community countries, potential political support for moves towards European integration. The British government should seek to mobilise this support.

The European Community has made provision for a review of progress towards the goals put forward in the Single European Act at the end of 1988 and at the end of 1990. Britain should play a constructive role in this review, rather than, as so often, barracking from the sidelines. We have at least as much to gain as any other member state of the Community from the liberalisation of trade, and, in particular, from the completion of the internal market. Indeed, it is in our interests to unfreeze the Community, since Britain remains, by contrast with France, a 'dissatisfied power'. The Common Agricultural Policy, agreed before Britain entered the Community, was hardly suited to our own economy, and we therefore joined a Community whose structure was weighted against us – an inevitable consequence, perhaps, of our unwillingness to join at the outset when the rules were being formulated. But now the rational strategy would be to cooperate with those member states which are seeking to reform the Community so that it can develop new common policies which might operate more to the advantage of Britain than the Common Agricultural Policy has done.

That this has not happened – that, indeed, Britain has taken the opposite stance – must be accounted as a supreme triumph of ideology over national self-interest. De Gaulle, for all his talk of French sovereignty, was perfectly prepared to pool it where that was to France's advantage. He froze the European Community after, not before, the passage of one major common policy – the Common Agricultural Policy – that was very much in France's national interest. It was perfectly understandable if De Gaulle felt that no further common policies, which might operate to the detriment of France, should be adopted. But British Gaullism would mean freezing the Community so that the only major common policy which it could sustain would be one that is inimical to our interests. Is there not some contradiction in being, like Margaret Thatcher, a British Gaullist?

When nations act irrationally, one must seek the cause in the dead weight of the past, in the persistence of habits of mind which have remained unquestioned for too long. It is our tradition of thinking about constitutional questions in terms of undivided sovereignty which inhibits a constructive approach to the development of the Community – and to devolution. For the concept of sovereignty implies that there must somewhere be a supreme political authority in the Community – either the member states, which means that Community decisions can be nothing more than the product of inter-governmental agreement; or the Community itself, and that involves the obliteration of the member states comprising the Community, the end, as Hugh Gaitskell once put it, of a thousand years of history. Yet there is a third alternative, a genuine division and sharing of power between the Community and the member states so that neither controls the other, but each undertakes only those tasks which it is best equipped to do. The whole history of the European Community shows that it is perfectly possible to *share* power, *divide* sovereignty so as to create a political entity capable of carrying out common policies without compromising the identity of the component units. Is our failure to appreciate this the result of anything more than a loss of constitutional and political imagination?

The Glorious Revolution of 1688 served to emphasise the undivided sovereignty of Parliament. The time has come to de-emphasise it.

Notes

1. I am grateful to Richard Corbett, Ralf Dahrendorf, Roy Jenkins, David Millar, John Pinder and Roy Pryce for their comments on an earlier draft of this chapter. But they are not to be implicated in my conclusions.
2. Jean Monnet, *Memoirs*, Collins, London, 1978, p. 377.
3. *The Europe We Joined*, BBC TV, October 1980.
4. David Marquand, *Parliament for Europe*, Jonathan Cape, London, 1979, p. 81.
5. Jean Monnet, *Memoirs*, op. cit., p. 513.
6. Hansard, House of Commons, 5 December 1985, col. 432.
7. I have analysed this proposal in more detail in an article, 'The Future of

the European Community: Two Models of Democracy' to be found in *Government and Opposition*, 1986.

III Redefining Citizenship

6 Bill of Rights and Law Reform

Lord Scarman

G. M. Trevelyan in his classic, *The History of England*,[1] wondered how glorious the 'Glorious Revolution' of 1688–89 really was. He suggested that 'there was indeed a certain ignominy in the fact that a foreign fleet and army, however friendly and however welcome, had been required to enable Englishmen to recover the liberties they had muddled away in their frantic faction feuds'.[2]

Macaulay, writing some 70 or so years earlier, was also struck by the peculiar character of the Revolution. It was very strange because, as he saw it, it changed almost nothing except the succession to the throne. 'It was', he said, 'a revolution strictly defensive, and had prescription and legitimacy on its side.' The main principles of our government were, in his view, already settled. In a famous passage he stated them:

> Our parliamentary institutions were in full vigour. The main principles of our government were excellent. They were not, indeed, formally and exactly set forth in a single written instrument: but they were to be found scattered over our ancient and noble statutes; and what was of far greater moment, they had been engraven on the hearts of Englishmen during four hundred years. That, without the consent of the representatives of the nation, no legislative act could be passed, no tax imposed, no regular soldiery kept up, that no man could be imprisoned, even for a day, by the arbitrary will of the sovereign, that no tool of power could plead the royal command as a justification for violating any right of the humblest subject, were held, both by Whigs and Tories, to be fundamental laws of the realm. A realm of which these were the fundamental laws stood in no need of a new constitution.[3]

Nevertheless he accepted that changes had to come. He found the evidence that they were needed in the fact that the constitution had not prevented royal misgovernment: 'there was somewhere a defect in our polity which it was the duty of the Convention [of 1688–89] to discover and supply'. His choice of words is significant: he had in mind a defect of omission.

Let Trevelyan have the last word. 'The true glory of the British Revolution lay in the fact that it was bloodless . . . and above all that a settlement by consent was reached.' He commented that 'the settlement of 1689 stood the test to time'.[4] And he made the point that the settlement was a landmark not only because of what it expressly provided but also because of the developments which followed as men began to translate its principles into action.

In 1988 we can agree with their judgement. The two historians accepted that the revolution of 1688–89 was necessary not because of any lack of principle in the constitution but because it had failed to prevent misgovernment. There was a defect of omission somewhere, which it was necessary to discover and to remedy.

The settlement between the Prince of Orange and the British Parliament, the tercentenary of which we shall be somewhat prematurely celebrating in 1988 (the Prince landed at Torbay on the 5 November 1688, but the settlement was not finally agreed until February 1689), was a reform designed to exclude any future opportunity for the Crown to run away with the government. The Settlement (I shall use the capital 'S' henceforward) tamed the King, diminishing his power to that of a constitutional monarch: it ensured the supremacy of the law over all: it declared and protected the independence of the judges: it reasserted the historic liberties of the English people: and it vested ultimate power in Parliament. The constitution remained unwritten in the sense explained by Macaulay: and its fundamental principle remained the rule of law.

These days we mock Filmer and those who with him believed in the divine right of the king. But the belief did at least spring from a deeply-implanted human instinct that the exercise of sovereign power within a community calls for a justification greater and more profound than the law itself can offer. The Romans looked to a *jus naturale*. A hundred or so years after the Settlement of 1688 the Europeans (and the Americans) were to resort to Locke and Rousseau for the concept of the rights of man which government was required to recognise and enforce. The same view has in the twentieth century come to the fore again in the human rights movement.

It is this belief that there are certain human rights and freedoms which no law may exclude, which is leading many in the United Kingdom to call for constitutional protection of the individual and of minorities and, indeed, of all the governed, against the power of the state.

The many honourable English people who in the seventeenth century believed in the divine right of the king at least recognised that kingly power needed the justification of divine authority. But they soon learnt that without constitutional checks and limits even divine authority could be abused. And when they could stand the abuse no longer, they looked to a constitutional settlement for their protection.

The Settlement achieved its purpose by putting the executive power of the state into a constitutional harness, placing the guiding reins firmly in the hands of Parliament. No departure from the constitutional principles of the past was needed or contemplated, but what was done was in truth a revolution. The enactment of changes in the succession to the throne really tells the whole story. Parliament accepted William not as Prince Consort vested with executive power but as King, though not he but his Queen was next in succession; and then in 1701 Parliament excluded the male Stuart line so as to transfer the succession to the protestant House of Hanover. Parliament thus asserted its right to determine who should be King. The monarch ruled no longer by divine but by constitutional right, and Parliament determined the constitution and the succession.

But, in taming the King, did we set in his place another absolute sovereign? If so, little was gained. In 1688 the answer to this question was 'no'. The Settlement avoided the trap, and at the same time achieved its legitimacy, by vesting supreme power in the Crown in Parliament. This was a genuine partnership, in the eighteenth century, of the executive and the legislature: for it could be said with truth that Parliament's supremacy was subject to a real restraint: the Crown had to be persuaded to agree. Inevitably, however, the partnership became more and more a formality: today, it is, of course, a ritual.

As the King became increasingly bound by convention and practice to act on the advice of ministers, so did Parliament come increasingly to take over the powers of government. Today the constitution and the law are what Parliament accepts or enacts. There is no constitutional ban on Parliament suspending habeas corpus, or restricting freedom of speech. The constitution provides no special protection for the constitution itself. There being no distinction between constitutional and other legislation, Parliament can as easily curtail or suspend our liberties as legislate to clean up the streets. The question becomes: have the democratic developments in the practice of our constitution resulted in the emergence of a parliamentary supremacy more complete even than the divine right of kings? And there is an even more disturbing question: is parliamentary supremacy, as now practised, really the supremacy of Parliament? Is it not in truth the supremacy of the executive? If this be so, the separation of powers will have broken down; the same group of people will be in control of the executive and the legislature; only the judges will retain their independence of the executive, but they will remain obliged by the 1688 Settlement to obey the legislation enacted by Parliament. The situation would indeed be one worthy of Lord Hailsham's cry of anguish: 'an elected dictatorship'.

The evidence that this situation has now arisen, namely that the executive is in command of the legislature with the judges sitting on the sidelines and unable to resist the combination of executive and legislative power, cannot, in any judgement, be denied. It has happened. It has been a gradual process. Not unnaturally for the first hundred years or so the Settlement of 1688 was seen as having finally established constitutional principle and practice. But today the evidence is that practice has departed from principle. The separation of powers has withered: a new executive has taken over two of the three powers of the state: the political party which forms the government is the new master of our polity.

The democratisation of our institutions has created this situation. But that is no argument against democratic development: it is, however, a reason for doubting whether the Settlement unamended can provide the citizens of our modern democratic state with the constitutional protection which they need against abuse of governmental power.

Some would dismiss this analysis as unduly depressing. Surely the political safeguards of our democratic process are such that we need not build into our constitution legal safeguards. Legal safeguards mean, inevitably, judicial review not only of executive action but of the constitutionality of legislation. Surely we do not want to confer on judges the power to invalidate legislation? Let's look at the evidence. Perhaps, there is today, as in different circumstances there was immediately before the 'Glorious Revolution' of 1688, a 'defect in our polity' which it is our duty to expose and to remedy.

The answer is to be found in the history of our constitutional development since 1688. Parliament has taken over from the Crown. The Crown is now the convenient, and ritually correct, word used to identify the executive power of the state. That power is exercised by a cabinet of ministers answerable to Parliament: and they themselves are members of Parliament.

The two Houses of Parliament have gone their different ways. The House of Commons is now the powerhouse: the House of Lords is limited almost entirely to an advisory and revising function: in almost all matters the House of Commons can enact laws notwithstanding the dissent of the House of Lords. The Commons are, however, an elected body, and a term (under existing law, five years) is set by law to the life of a parliament, after which a general election has to be called. Of course elections may be held more frequently, and usually are: but an earlier election is a matter for the decision of the Prime Minister in office at the time and is usually determined by considerations of party advantage. Elections are based on universal suffrage, the vote is secret; and the party which gains, or can achieve by political negotiation, an overall majority assumes control of the executive and legislative powers of the state. The constitutional separation of these powers as between the Crown and Parliament no longer represents reality. Parliament is supreme: it has become a genuinely democratic body, but it is itself controlled and managed by the political party in power.

The House of Lords has declined in power, but perhaps not in influence. It does retain the power to prevent a House of Commons from extending its own life. It is our only legal safeguard against an 'elected dictatorship'. But it is itself an unelected body. Its members are part hereditary, part appointed (life peers), part temporal (hereditary and life peers), part spiritual (the bishops of the Church of England, or more accurately some of them). The Parliament Acts of 1911 and 1949 have enabled the House of Commons to legislate without its assent, the Lords are able to delay but not to prevent legislation proposed by the Commons. Its true function is now review and revision which the Commons may at pleasure accept or reject.

Legislation can, however, still be introduced in the House of Lords, and frequently is. This is a valuable initiative which the House retains, though the House of Commons holds the power of final legislative decision. For instance, the House of Lords has twice passed through all its stages a Bill to introduce into British law the guarantees of human rights and fundamental freedoms which the United Kingdom, by ratifying the European Convention of Human Rights and Fundamental Freedoms, has undertaken to provide to all who are within the Kingdom. But the Commons has declined the invitation to enact the Bill: and so there is no Act of Parliament incorporating the Convention into our law.

The House of Lords retains, as I have already mentioned, one essential power: its assent is required to any extension of the period of five years after which a new House of Commons has to be elected. The House of Commons cannot, under existing law, prolong its own life beyond five years without the assent of the House of Lords. But even this safeguard could be removed if a House of Commons should act in time to get the necessary legislation through without the Lords' assent.

The risk, then, is of an 'elected dictatorship'. The party which can command a majority in the House of Commons controls the executive and legislative powers of the state. It reigns supreme because Parliament is supreme. Is the risk sufficiently great so as to rank as a 'defect in our polity' which we should 'supply' by constitutional reform? I believe that it is. Like the English parliamentarians of 1688, I would settle for reform in place of revolution. Or, if you choose to call my proposal revolution, it is at least a revolution of a very 'peculiar character'. For it can be achieved without breaking the continuity of the constitution.

I suggest constitutional reform for two reasons. First, we must now protect individual human rights and liberties, and the rights of minorities who cannot in the foreseeable future expect to attain political power, from the abuse of state power which is possible under the constitution. As I have shown, there were in 1688 greater constitutional restraints upon the abuse of parliamentary power than there are today. The Crown and the House of Lords were then a powerful restraint upon the House of Commons: the two Houses were a powerful restraint upon the Crown: and the two Houses, being equal and separate, ensured that neither enjoyed legislative sovereignty. All these restraints on the elected majority in the House of Commons have withered away. The weakness of the 1688 Settlement was its lack of democratic content. Parliament existed and was strengthened; but its electorate was limited, elections were stained by corruption; and, when elected, it was of less consequence than the House of Lords. It took nearly 200 years to achieve a House of Commons truly representative of the people. This leads me to reflect on the major weakness of the Settlement of 1688, its defects of omission. The lack of democratic content has been made good by the Reform Act of 1832 and subsequent legislation. But the other serious omissions continue to enfeeble the constitution.

DEFECTS OF OMISSION

The Settlement of 1688 was not seen by those who drew it up as a new constitution. England already had, in their view, an excellent constitutional protection of our liberties in the combination of the common law, developed by the judges and the great statutes such as Magna Carta and the Habeas Corpus laws enacted by Parliament over the centuries. The view was: tame the King, and the constitution is rid of its defect and stands in all its nobility. But we now know that the principle of the common law that we are free to do whatever we wish so long as it is lawful needs supplementing. It fails to deal, for example, with racial discrimination or sexual inequality: it does not restrict the power of Parliament to limit freedom of speech or of the press: it offers no protection of privacy or family life: and it is unable to protect the rights of minorities.

The case for an Act of Parliament incorporating into our law the rights and freedoms guaranteed by the European Convention of Human Rights and Fundamental Freedoms is that it would remedy the omissions of our existing law. Such an Act is to be welcomed, if it comes. But it would not supply the constitutional omission. An Act of Parliament can be amended or repealed whenever 'Parliament', in reality the political party controlling the House of Commons, chooses. The modern constitution lacks even the safeguards of 1688.

Another defect of omission is the lack of constitutional protection of minorities. The common law has had to be supplemented by legislation. We have legislation covering racial and sex equality and outlawing discrimination on the grounds of race, colour, origin, religion, or sex. But a House of Commons, if determined to repeal such legislation or some part of it, could not be prevented from doing so. The unavoidable conclusion is that our existing constitution has no protection to offer against abuse of power by Parliament. Such safeguards as have existed, the Crown itself at first and the House of Lords, are now shadows of their former selves. And there are, of course, no judicial restraints upon the power of Parliament.

REFORM

I suggest that we should now, before it is too late, prepare proposals for a written constitution based on the separation of powers; declaring the rights and liberties to be constitutionally protected; establishing a supreme constitutional court with jurisdiction to review executive and legislative action to ensure that it is within the limits set by the constitution; and requiring special procedures for the amendment of the constitution.

Such a programme would take time. A Royal Commission would, no doubt, be proposed: the opportunities for delay would be legion.

I would suggest, therefore, two interim measures which would achieve much, although more is needed. They are:

(1) a Bill of Rights based on the European Convention of Human Rights (to which the United Kingdom is a party): the House of Lords has already expressly approved such a Bill;
(2) a new Parliamentary Act requiring the assent of *both* Houses of Parliament to the amendment of certain scheduled Acts of Parliament; and
(3) the Schedule to the Act should include the new Bill of Rights, all legislation promoting racial equality and equal rights for women, the structural legislation establishing local government, and other legislation, notably the Habeas Corpus Acts and Magna Carta, considered to be of constitutional importance.

I accept, of course, that the House of Lords itself should be reformed. Its present membership is not sufficiently democratic in character, though the members are proving themselves effective and vigilant champions of the rights of individuals and of minorities. Perhaps, if we strengthen the House's powers, Parliament will recognise the need to reform its membership.

These measures would not give us a constitutional court, which we sadly lack; but they would reinstate in an altered form the separation of Parliament and of powers which existed under the 1688 Settlement before the King and the House of Lords were relegated almost exclusively to an advisory role, but would greatly diminish the dangers of oppression by (as Lord Hailsham put it, echoing Jefferson when the Americans were building a constitution based on common law principles) an 'elected dictatorship'.

But our ultimate goal must remain: a constitution which is based on a true and legally enforceable separation of the powers of the government, which declares and defines our constitutional rights and freedoms, and which establishes a court having jurisdiction on challenge by any person or group of persons to review the constitutionality of executive action and legislation and to give the appropriate relief if either be held to be contrary to the constitution.

Notes

1. G. M. Trevelyan, *The History of England*, Longman, London, 1926.
2. Ibid., p. 472.
3. T. B. Macaulay, *The History of England*, Vol. II, Chapter X, fr. 571, The World's Classics, Oxford University Press, Oxford, 1931 edition.
4. Trevelyan, *History of England*, op. cit., p. 472.

7 Citizenship and the Modern Social Conflict

Ralf Dahrendorf

The politics of liberty is about more life chances for more people. Its condition and constitutional basis is civil society. A civil society is a society of citizens in the full sense of the word. Many countries have a long way to go to this goal. Citizenship is the theme of changes in the Soviet Union, the desire of many in Eastern Europe, the imperative need in South Africa and in the remaining dictatorships of Latin America, the great task in the developing world. But citizenship is under pressure in the developed free countries – the OECD countries – as well. It is certainly under pressure in Britain. It is therefore well to remember what it means and to consider the next steps towards the constitution of civil society.

Citizenship is a set of entitlements which are common to every member of society. Every member? There are exceptions, young children for example, or those who for a time had to be deprived of their citizenship rights on grounds of mental illness or delinquency. It is a liberal principle to keep such disenfranchisement to a minimum. The smaller the number of members of a society is who do not enjoy full civil rights, the more freedom exists. Moreover, those who are deprived of full citizenship must be protected from exploitation and abuse.

This principle applies also when it comes to defining 'members'. We have grown accustomed to regarding those who were born of parents domiciled in a national territory as members of a society, but the definition has important ambiguities as well as problematic limits. The most important question is that of the 'territory' itself which seems to define citizenship. I shall argue that the principle of civil society requires that there be a world civil society at the end of the road. (Immanuel Kant, in his occasional papers on 'Eternal Peace' and on 'Universal History with Cosmopolitan Intent' was the first, more than two hundred years ago, to make this point.) But unless and until this dream becomes real, civil societies exist within national boundaries, because nations are the guarantors – or destroyers – of the rule of law. Thus 'citizens' have to be 'nationals' which raises not only the question of multinational parentage, or of residence and domicile, but above all that of refugees. In a century in which more people are on the move across boundaries than ever before, this is a fundamental question of citizenship. Some seek political asylum, others mere survival, again others an improvement in their social and economic conditions, many are pushed about by arbitrary rulers and rules, and all these millions desire full citizenship rights in vain. I shall return to their story.

First there is the definition of citizenship in a substantive rather than a territorial sense. The key word in this context is entitlement. In the 1980s, this is not exactly a widely appreciated word. Many prefer to speak of obligations, sometimes to the detreiment of civil society. If for no other reason, it is important to revive interest in the concept. Entitlements are rights which are intended to be removed from the caprices of day-to-day politics. Such rights may be entrenched in constitutions, or sufficiently time-honoured to defy easy change; they may even be purely factual conditions which have come to be accepted as right. Free speech is an example of the former, a certain level of real wages one of the latter, and in between there are many other entitlements which will be discussed presently. (Whether certain opportunities of access and participation are an entitlement or not is itself a subject of political debate and thus of historical change.) All citizens are entitled to do certain things. They have certain basic rights and guaranteed opportunities. They can leave and re-enter their country, for example (and if they cannot, they are subjects rather than citizens); they can speak their minds, cast their votes for one of several candidates for office. Perhaps they can even live a decent life.

The last two centuries have seen tidal swings in prevailing views of what entitlements citizenship should include. For a long time – and for good reasons – the main subject was one of extending civil rights in the narrow sense of this term. The great civic revolutions established that no one should be above the law. This marks an enormous step forward from the notion that 'by the grace of God' some are entitled to push others around; it is therefore hardly surprising that equality before the law is still not universally realised even in the most civilised societies. Time and again someone arrogates to himself or herself unusual powers, and some simply grab such powers without much ado. Reminders that no one is above the law are one of the great tasks of the courts. The civic revolutions also established the right of every citizen to conclude free contracts and to invoke public power when they are not honoured. Such contracts are the basis of capitalist economies in more ways than one. Markets and exchanges rely on contract; in this sense the right to contract means freedom. But this right also includes the contract of labour, and as long as one side has to sell work whereas the other may or may not buy it, it is a caricature of freedom. Even so, it is preferable both to pre-modern dependence and to forced labour.

The reason is that the weaknesses of the labour market can be remedied within the context of citizenship. Historically, the imbalance of the labour contract was corrected by organisation, notably by trade unions, and to some extent by legislation ('labour law'). This required a second stage in the development of modern civil societies which was that of political entitlements. (The notion of stages should not be taken too seriously; history and the logic of history are not the same, and in many countries political rights preceded civil rights.) As civil rights constitute the market, political rights constitute the public, that is the marketplace of participating citizens. One is talking about rights of participation which include freedom of association and freedom of speech, but also arrangements for translating the views of citizens into decisions, or at least control of decisions. Suffrage has been the great theme of political citizenship rights, and from the suffragettes to the American civil (and voting) rights movement it has mobilised people.

Civil and political rights are relatively uncontested elements of citizenship (though in practice they are much more complicated than strikes the eye). But as T. H. Marshall has shown, in his splendid study *Citizenship and Social Class*,[1] the twentieth-century theme was that of social citizenship rights. What entitlements of social position should every citizen enjoy in a civilised society? The need is easy to see. Equality before the law means little if some can afford to use lawyers and courts to advance their interests and others cannot. Even suffrage, let alone freedom of speech are mere promises for those who have no knowledge or information about issues and parties. In any case, citizenship means too little for people who are left to their own often insufficient resources in illness and old age. The Welfare State is the response of many modern societies to this deficiency. (Many, but not all: most Americans still believe that given civil and political rights, people should be able to stand on their own feet; though the American Dream has been tempered by Social Security for the retired, Medicare and Medicaid for the majority, and other measures.) The notion of welfare is misleading. Its patronising connotations detract from the fact that it is about entitlements. Pensions and medical care, insurance against accidents, but also education and perhaps a minimum wage are civil rights, not charitable gifts.

However, this is precisely where the tide has begun to turn in recent years. Full citizenship may include civil, political and social entitlements – but how many of the latter? How much social citizenship can we afford? At what point are social entitlements no longer entry tickets to full participation but deterrents from participation? Do they not create a new kind of dependency, that of welfare families rather than self-reliant citizens? Is it not necessary therefore in the interest of an effective civil society to roll back the nannying welfare state and seek a new constitutional settlement which reminds us of the minimal needs of government action? Is not the new social contract a set of basic rights and rules of the game rather than a hodgepodge of entitlements?

These are the great questions of the 1980s. Before I turn to them, three footnotes about citizenship are in place. It will be clear by now that citizenship is a principle of equality. It defines what all members of society have in common. It is a common status. Yet status is too static a notion to indicate what it is about. Citizenship is an entry ticket; it provides access. This raises the complicated problems of equality of results *versus* equality of opportunity, which we can leave on one side here. But the question must be answered of what the entry ticket is for, and to what access is provided. My answer is, to choices among what I call provisions. Entitlements are opportunities to share in the diverse and varied world of provisions, whether material or organisational or whatever. Goods and services are provisions, but so are political parties and schools and kinds of medical service. A free society will offer both full citizenship rights for all and a wide range of options of material and immaterial provisions. It might even be argued that there are times when entitlements are the main subject of conflict, and times when it is provisions. Many seem to believe that the 1980s are a time for extending choices. They tend to overlook the price in citizenship which is paid for this preference. Ideally, liberal politics is about changes which enhance both access and choice. Maynard Keynes's notion of 'effective demand' was an example in its time; basic income guarantees may be one today.

There is no implication here that provisions should be distributed equally. The point about full citizenship – and this is the second footnote – is that it transforms social conflicts from all-or-nothing battles into a mechanism to bring about gradual change. As long as insuperable entitlement barriers are the issue, conflicts are a zero-sum game. One side has to give way and will lose what the other side gains. Inequalities have an absolute and therefore unbearable character. South Africa's problem tells the story. Once citizenship rights are established, conflicts are about more or less of things which are in principle accessible to everybody. Perhaps this is what the many theorists of the 1950s and 1960s had in mind who were talking about the 'institutionalisation of class conflict' (Th. Geiger), or the 'democratic class struggle' (S. M. Lipset), or were even advancing an 'economic theory of democracy' (A. Downs) according to which political parties had become like companies competing for a market, except that their success is counted in votes rather than in dollars. These and other authors were over-optimistic (if that is the word). History never stands still. As soon as one set of entitlement problems is largely resolved, another one arises. This too is a theme of the 1980s.

This has much to do with the subject of a third footnote. Entitlements are all very well (some would argue), but what about the other side, obligations? Is not citizenship a contract which involves both rights and duties? What does the individual give to others for the entitlements of citizenship? At least one author (L. Mead) has made this the central point of his plea, in a book called *Beyond Entitlements*,[2] to remember obligation as the first priority of the next stage of social and political development; many politicians would undoubtedly agree with him. Yet there is something seriously misleading about this view which has to be clarified.

I find it pleasing to see the old notion of a social contract revived in contemporary political theory. It draws attention to the principles underlying any constitutional settlement. These are not necessarily an unchanging set of maxims and rules, from the integrity of the person to the due process of law. The content of the social contract is itself subject to historical change. The social contract is forever a task before us. Some authors have failed to see this dynamic quality and instead produced a straitjacket which limits liberty rather than promoting it. As I understand it, the social contract embodies the underlying assumptions of societies at a particular time and place. They give life to constitutional arrangements; they are as it were the spirit of the laws. Citizenship is certainly a part of the modern social contract.

Yet there is one sense in which the word 'contract' is misleading; that is, the allusion to the private contract to which I referred earlier. A private contract is based on mutuality, on give-and-take, in that sense on rights and obligations. The social contract, on the other hand, defines the common floor on which everybody stands. Some believe that it should therefore stipulate that people actually have to stand rather than sit or lie about. Several countries have introduced compulsory voting for this reason. In most countries, there is a view about that opportunities must be used, as a matter of moral if not of legal duty. If political parties are there, people should take an interest in them; if educational opportunities are general, intelligent youngsters should aspire to A-levels; if certain social services to which people are entitled are not used, one has to inform people of their rights. I find these notions wrong and even repugnant. In a sense, the right not to make use of opportunities is the real issue. Entitlements are chances; turning them into duties takes away their most precious element of freedom.

Are there then no obligations attached to citizenship? Two spring to mind immediately. One is to comply with the law, and the other is to pay taxes. Both are clearly acceptable, indeed necessary, though there are good reasons why they have been the subject of theoretical and practical political debate for centuries. This is notably true for taxes. 'No taxation without representation' sounds fine – but what about the reverse? Should those who pay no taxes be allowed to vote? Today we tend to say yes, precisely because we assume the absolute character of certain entitlements, like suffrage; but this was not always the prevailing response, and there may well be a case for constructing a system of taxation which includes everybody either positively, as a taxpayer, or negatively, as a recipient of 'negative income tax'. The point is that the basic social contract is one of equals. This is incidentally why the recent libertarian debate in America about progressive taxation is so important, and why the income tax reform which reduces multiple tax rates to two is so remarkable. If taxation is an obligation associated with citizenship, what justification is there for taxing some more highly than others?

Citizenship is a status common to all members of society. The metaphor of the social contract must not deter from the fact that it is above all a set of entitlements, rights. Rights lose their quality if they become conditional. (The encroachment of economic thinking on the law, from plea bargaining to income-related penalties endangers the rule of law.) Insofar as there are duties or obligations of citizens these must be thought of as equally universal. All citizens have to comply with the law (which raises the difficult issue of the position of 'apprentice-citizens' who are under age but responsible for many violent crimes). All citizens have to pay taxes (which raises the issues at which I have hinted above). If there is a tax on time, such as conscription, all citizens should be subject to it (which raises the issue of women's military service which is alive in several countries). By the same token, work – the central concern of the author of *Beyond Entitlement* and indeed of many not only in the United States – cannot be thought of as an obligation of all citizens. The subject is important because it raises central questions of welfare reform, such as 'workfare' and youth employment schemes. Work involves essentially private contracts, which means that it cannot be traded against citizenship rights. Requiring work in exchange for basic entitlements comes close to the advocacy of forced labour. (The limiting case of community service is in any case a version of conscription.) In a free society, the right not to work is the more important principle. This is not to say that the availability of work is a matter of indifference. People's livelihood, self-respect, and even transfer incomes are likely to depend on work for some time to come. But it is to say that citizenship rights, and the social contract, stipulate unconditional entitlements, and that any condition detracts from their quality.

The subject of work takes us back to the new entitlement problems of the 1980s, and therefore to the tasks of citizenship today and tomorrow. Poverty is as old as mankind. Unemployment is a much more recent notion; when it was discovered as such in the late nineteenth century, people were deeply shocked; but of course underemployment which is so widespread in the developing world today was no less general in the countries of today's OECD world. Perhaps it can be said that in the last hundred years there has been a secular trend to reduce poverty and unemployment, though such a blanket statement flies in the face of flagrant exceptions in certain regions and at certain times. Certainly in the postwar decades two things have happened together. One is the reduction in the number of people who actually fall below the poverty line, and also the decline in the number of unemployed. (There is the vexing subject of 'relative deprivation' which in my view raises provisions rather than entitlement issues, but which cannot be pursued here.) The other trend is for issues of poverty and unemployment to become manageable 'within the system', as it were. Boundaries became tenuous; people went in and out of poverty; acceptable policy measures actually reached the poor and the unemployed.

The 1970s changed this picture. They were in any case a decade of profound and as yet unrecognised changes. Stagflation raised doubts in the ability of advanced countries to go on deploying the instruments needed for coping with deprivation. When the cycle was eventually broken, and modest (sometimes not so modest) growth under conditions of low, even zero-inflation returned, the price turned out to be high. It is important to avoid the mistake made by many social and economic analysts in the 1970s of overstating immediate developments. The 1980s are just about to end, and there is no telling at this stage how many of their features will soon look very ephemeral indeed. Certainly the German Greens look as if they are going to leave the political stage with a whimper. The stockmarket crash of 19 October makes one wonder how long casino capitalism is going to last. Even Thatcherism may turn out to have been an episode, albeit a consequential one. Even so, the cost of a decade obsessed with provisions and oblivious of entitlements – a decade of growth without citizenship – will be evident for some time to come. It will certainly be evident for the victims.

The central fact which comes to mind is that these days economic growth – the growth of provisions – seems to be possible without a portion of the population being involved at all. This is not new, nor is it unique. Many developing countries have gone through phases in which a minority benefited from economic development while the majority was left out of it. Nicaragua is the last of several examples of the consequences. What is new is that the majority benefits or can hope to benefit whereas a minority is defined out. This has happened in many OECD countries. In most parts of Europe, long-term unemployment is the result. Those who have employment have a reasonable income which is fairly 'sticky' in Keynes's sense, that is it does not decline despite growing unemployment or even dips in conjunctural fortunes. Those, on the other hand, who do not have employment are less and less likely to find it. They are not needed, or so it appears. Having low skills in the first place, and often other disadvantages, they also become less and less employable. In the United States, employment is not the major issue. Spectacular increases in the number of jobs available put Europeans to shame. But many of the new jobs are poorly paid and insecure. Even apart from a residue of permanently unemployed, and from destitute one-parent families, a category of 'working poor' has emerged which in many ways corresponds to the long-term unemployed in Europe.

The key point is that these are people whose position of disadvantage can apparently no longer be remedied by the normal operation of the economic and political process. The word 'underclass' is understandably disputed by many. One is clearly not talking about a class in the strict sense of the term. There are also very considerable differences between the ghettoes of American inner cities (which W. J. Wilson writes about) and the pockets of extreme deprivation in most European countries, though Britain is a halfway house in this respect as in others. But there are signs that a certain percentage of the citizens of OECD countries get caught in a cycle of deprivation which it becomes harder and harder to break. What percentage? Estimates vary considerably. Some say that one is concerned with a hard core of one per cent, others argue that 15 per cent are in an underclass position. Even 5 per cent would be a significant figure to describe those who do not enjoy the entitlements of citizenship which are meant to be general in civil societies.

A brief sketch of this kind begs some questions and leaves many others unanswered. Neither in Europe nor in the United States is it as yet certain that people cannot break out of the cycle of deprivation without radical changes in structure. It is doubtful whether the problem has reached constitutional dimensions yet. But it is close to doing so. A significant portion of all citizens are at least pushed to the margin and perhaps defined out. There are many views as to why this has happened. Some point to changes in the role of work with which I started this argument. Others believe that in due course, normal economic processes will deal. Again others think that the welfare state itself is responsible for the new deprivation. It has robbed (they say) people of the motivation which they need in order to get out of the rut. It is a pity that while there are many inconclusive causal analyses, few have looked at success stories. Some people have made it despite adversity, and they tell us not only that they are clever, but also what it was that was required to break the cycle.

I have a view about this question which may well provide at least a partial answer to the new problems of citizenship. It may even help define a set of principles which can guide the reform of the welfare state. The immediate reason why some manage to break out of the cycle of deprivation has to do with human motives. While many have settled down to the miseries of poverty and helplessness, some begin to grasp new and different opportunities. This is often due to unusual circumstances. Dramatic events shake up the habit of destitution, as the earthquake did in the vast slums of Mexico City. Charismatic individuals sometimes achieve the same result. A priest who makes the welfare of one-parent families in his parish his special concern, an imaginative chairman of a housing estate who mobilises people against crime and the deterioration of the stock, an employer who offers attractive rewards for educational achievement – these and others can get through to people whose lethargy seemed as bad as their actual condition.

This may not look much like a social policy, let alone one of citizenship; it is almost the invocation of a *deus ex machina* to clear up the mess. Yet such a conclusion would be as mistaken as the inference that charismatic leadership or other unusual events are all that is needed. They clearly are critical, but they are not sufficient. What is needed to deal with persistent unemployment or persistent poverty is really a combination of several things: the spark of hope which is preferably not ignited by an earthquake but by an unusual person; a community (family?) readiness to help which goes far beyond what has come to be customary and includes care for children, for the sick and the elderly; and an effective system for transferring the necessary resources. Many mistakes have been made in organising social citizenship rights, and in the inevitable reforms at least some of them should be undone, but the principle remains valid that every citizen is entitled to the security of a basic status which is independent of his or her market value. This requires money.

The questions are: how much? how should it be raised? and how should it be made available? Citizenship demands a system which is universal, non-discriminatory, and simple. In other words, neither elaborate methods of targeting nor the creation of numerous pots for different needs, nor the setting up of a huge bureaucracy are compatible with the intended effect. This is why basic income guarantees and negative income tax mechanisms are so attractive. They may have been dismissed in the United States as a result of large-scale experiments from which some have concluded that their side-effects on motivation are undesirable; but this is not to say that a viable method cannot be found. Such a method need not aim at providing a guarantee for the level of funding required for a civilised existence. It is more important that whatever level is guaranteed has a constitutional quality and is not subject to frequent changes on transparent political grounds. In any case, it is one lesson of the 1970s that we must combine income transfers with a greater encouragement of individuals to look after themselves. This is where work, work-related insurance schemes, as well as measures to encourage work and make it worthwhile, have their place. The result would be a combination of a basic income guarantee, a (possibly subsidised) individual contribution, and a greater emphasis on solidarity in communities – not a bad prescription for a modern notion of social citizenship.

Once again, the subject demands footnotes in the absence of extensions. One of them has to do with the question of who will press for a new social contract in the narrower sense of the reconstruction of the welfare state. In whose interest are the changes at which I have hinted? The political significance of the question is obvious. Unless support for a new contract of citizenship can be found, nothing will happen. There will be innumerable small adjustments which are likely to aggravate the position of those who are no longer on board. Yet it is hard to see why the possessing majority of those who find current circumstances quite satisfactory, to realise their aspirations should press for change.

There is no simple answer, except that clearly the social basis of modern politics has changed. The age of class politics is over, and issue politics relies in the nature of the case on mobilising different people in different situations. In this particular case, the need is for the mobilisation of moral minorities. By that I mean those people who are moved by the plight of the deprived and excluded, for whatever reason. They are quite likely to be people also who do not wish to see public action confined to the immediate and the short-term, but want to be sure that the world in which they are living has some long-term stability. From this point of view their motives may even be described as interests rather than mere flights of moral fancy.

Both the moral minority and the recipe for dealing with the underclass have relevance for a much larger issue which is nonetheless related, the issue of development in the Third World. I can but hint at it here, though there is no doubt about the relevance of the subject. Indeed, the mistakes made in policies towards the Third World have much in common with those of the welfare state. There was a time of large-scale transfers of resources which failed to have the desired effect. There was then a degree of targeting, of projects financed and supervised by international bureaucracies, which often did not reach the people for whom they were intended. Today, a much more modest community-based approach has gained currency, though it is often pursued without the necessary back-up in resources.

It could be argued that the initial purpose of policies of development should be the creation of civil societies everywhere. This involves human rights and political checks and balances, but it involves above all the ability of a growing number of people to take part in the markets and the public of their countries. Charismatic leadership at the local level has a great deal to do with this objective. One successful cooperative venture in a village of seventy or eighty farmers can be more effective than building twenty dams which are not accepted by anybody. The work of young, and not-so-young people from the First World in the villages and towns of the Third World deserves much more praise than it gets. But again, some form of aid through an IMF–World Bank system is a necessary part of the process of creating effective civil societies everywhere.

The argument for a world civil society is in part moral. If all human beings are equal in their humanity, then constitutional arrangements which bring out the best in people must not be a privilege. As usual, the moral is not altogether remote from the practical. Civil societies cannot easily survive in isolation, especially not at a time at which such isolation would have to be a deliberate act of self-insulation. It is true that Britain has done rather well in preserving and developing its civil society, as has the United States, and perhaps more to the point in geographical terms, Switzerland. (The imperfections of all of them cannot detract from the fact that the momentum of citizenship was present throughout the last centuries.) But defensive civil societies are at risk of becoming less civil. There is a link between citizenship, confidence and liberty which works the other way as well: once anxiety, protectionism and isolationism, or mere insularity set in, civil rights too are soon under pressure. In a world of close interrelations those who cease to espouse the cause of a world civil society put their own civility at risk.

These observations are relevant for a final comment which must temper the relative optimism of this discussion of citizenship and the modern social conflict. It is by no means certain that the time has come for a new constitutional settlement or social contract. The old settlement began to collapse in the 1970s. Here and there, ideas for a new settlement have been launched. But so far the moral minority has remained very much a minority, and one which tends to be dismissed rather than followed.

The main reason is that the possessing majority feels under threat and reacts like most people who are anxious and defensive, that is by closing ranks and protecting what they have got. Along with trade protectionism a kind of social protectionism has emerged which aims at keeping people out rather than bringing them in. Worse, some of those who were in are pushed to the margin and beyond, whereas none of those who might have a claim to becoming a part of things are allowed that privilege. Privilege? They are not allowed to be citizens, that is to share the entitlements of membership. This is how the underclass may come about at a time at which the majority looks to a new burst in provisions (albeit one of the casino variety). This is how the Third World is allowed to sink deeper into the quagmire of poverty and tyranny.

But perhaps the most worrying sign of social protectionism is the extent to which many seem to find it difficult in the 1980s to accept that people of different creed or race or colour can and should have equal rights. Citizenship which is a great force for making differences fruitful for all, is used to attack heterogeneity and to support homogeneous groups. Historically, it is surely one of the great riddles of our time that with all our experience and all our wealth we seem unable to accept as fellow-citizens those who are culturally different from us. Worse, some of the cruellest battles of the time are fought, at great cost of human lives to say nothing of happiness, over the question of who belongs and who does not. The tidal wave of citizenship has not only swung back from the social rights of all, but from the extension of membership as well. This is, in Karl Popper's sense, a time of returning to the tribe rather than going forward to the open society.

Some believe that the way to fight this trend is to counter it in its own language and make simple cases for simple values. I disagree. One theme of citizenship, and of the modern social conflict today is complexity, and heterogeneity. These are not very attractive words, and others could be found to make the same case. There are virtues in difference, and in appreciating that the world is not simple, certainly the world of liberty is not. Citizenship is an instrument for uniting the diverse without destroying diversity. Just as it is compatible with social inequalities as long as they do not destroy opportunities for participation of others, it is compatible also with cultural differences which are contained by the common commitment to a civil society. The old enemy of citizenship was privilege, and total deprivation; the new enemy may well be fundamentalism. In any case, it is clear that we still have, and may forever have a long way to go to civil society.

Notes

1. T. H. Marshall, *Citizenship and Social Class*, Cambridge University Press, Cambridge, 1950.
2. Lawrence M. Mead, *Beyond Entitlement*, Free Press, New York, 1986.

IV Revitalising Democracy

8 Parties, Parliament and PR

Richard Holme

Not least of the problems of a discussion of electoral reform in Britain is to establish that the issue is one of constitutional principle, a first-order question, rather than simply being a secondary question of mechanical adjustment.

Should electoral systems be considered to belong in the constitutional domain? In two countries which use proportional representation systems, the evidence points in different directions in so far as the written constitution is concerned. In the postwar Federal Republic of Germany, for instance, the compromise two-vote proportional representation system, although much commented upon in all analysis of the relative success of the post-Hitler settlement, did not form part of the *Grundgezetz*, or basic constitutional law, and indeed post-dated it.

By contrast, in Eire, another country which uses PR, in this instance the single transferable vote in multi-member constituencies, the electoral system is a part of the constitution which like other entrenched provisions can only be changed by a constitutional referendum.

Even if Britain had a written constitution, it could by no means be assumed that the electoral system would form part of it, although some generalised principles relating to frequency of elections, the secrecy of the ballot and the universal basis of the suffrage would almost certainly find a place within its pages.

Nevertheless much of the debate about the British electoral system, and alternatives to it, does takes place at a fundamental constitutional level. The electoral system is treated as an aspect of the constitutional way in which we do things, as a constitutionalist issue. Judgements are regularly made of the relative capacity of various systems to provide certain political 'goods' such as J. S. Mill's idea[1] of *the educative effect* of democracy on the voter, *legitimacy* of the legislature, *fairness* of outcome, *participation* in the process, *choice* of representatives, or *efficacy* of government. This latter good is often described as 'strong government' by the advocates of the status quo.

Alongside these arguments of constitutional principle and often overlapping with them in debate, are the detailed mechanical questions which are the bones and sinews of any system of inputs and outputs: the basis of the constituency; the format of the ballot-paper; and the method of counting. This chapter does not deal, except incidentally, with these mechanical issues but concentrates instead on the effect of alternative voting systems on the political process.

However, there is also a third category of debate which in practice tends to swamp the other two. It is the effect of the system upon the parties. Electoral reform in this context is judged not by its effect on the voters or on the nature of democratic government but by the calculation of which parties might gain from a new system and which might lose.

This narrow assessment of party gains and loss may be inevitable given that all parties will inevitably be affected one way or another by electoral reform. Moreover there is a general tendency in the British political culture for issues of the public interest to be trimmed down to partisan size. Such reductionism should be resisted as far as possible in considering electoral reform for, in considering the merits of alternative electoral systems, partisanship cannot be an adequate criterion. For instance the argument that it is for the government alone to decide the electoral system should be compared with the fact that an independent boundary commission is used to delimit constituency boundaries. Why? Because the government – any government – has an interest in the outcome of their deliberations.

Most political systems contrive to recognise the difference between the zealous prosecution of the game by the rival political sides and the rules of the game itself. In Britain, where the rules are few and not written down, this distinction is proving increasingly difficult to draw. The game overflows the boundaries. So in a British context much of the debate about reform can only proceed on an 'as if' basis; as if there were basic constitutional rules which could be modified in a prescribed way and the support for which transcended the ebb and flow of party advantage.

It is on this 'as if' basis that the electoral system deserves scrutiny; as if it had the character of a basic rule of the constitution which, because it contains values and assumptions about government and society, helps to determine the way our democracy works. Such rules might be thought to deserve specially respectful treatment.

It should be recognised that this approach is essentially conservative in that it sets a higher standard of consent for change and erects greater obstacles to reform than a purely mechanical adjustment might require. On the other hand, in the kingdom of 'as if', consideration of the electoral system and its reform would be possible not only in the adversarial cockpit but in the public forum.

In such a debate, the 'goods' which the traditional first-past-the-post system might be said to represent and to help deliver are by no means negligible. First, it is claimed to produce a strong competitive two-party system, in which the 'Outs' can and do replace the 'Ins' at regular intervals. Second, there is constituency representation which earths Parliament in the localities of the country. This allows an older British notion of democracy, the boroughs and shires coming to Westminster, to continue and coexist with a modern party system which is rooted more in minds than in places. Third, the electoral system produces a government with a majority adequate to pass its legislation and thus 'strong'. Fourth, once in place, the government is faced by an opposition playing its parliamentary role of criticising and contending with the Executive and all the while preparing for the moment not too far distant when roles will be reversed.

The virtues of the present system might thus be summarised as choice, representation, strong government and clear opposition. At this point it begins to become clear that the electoral system is indeed a first-order constitutional question since these virtues are intrinsic to the traditional description of the British party and parliamentary system, and it is the electoral system which is in large part their guarantor.

Yet how well do those claimed virtues stand up to inspection, for they may not be all they seem, or even if they are, they may not be properly guaranteed by the system?

The choice offered by the two-party system needs closer scrutiny for it is a severely limited choice. The winner-takes-all voting method might have been expressly designed to maintain electoral duopoly so high are the barriers which it erects to the entry of a third party. For a third party to become a viable choice it has first to become half of the duopoly, forcing whichever duopolist it replaces out of the 'either-or' decision frame. This can happen in a small way regionally but for it to happen nationally, the third party has effectively to surmount the barrier of one-third of the votes polled to get ahead of the erstwhile second party. In short the parties may change places, as they did when Labour replaced the Liberals in the 1920s, but the supremacy of the two-party system will remain intact.

A choice which lies between two alternatives only seems unduly restricted on any comparative basis with other democracies. In continental Europe there is invariably a wider choice of parties available to the voters, part cause and part effect of the different voting systems which those countries employ. In countries like Canada, Australia and New Zealand, whose political systems are based on the Westminster model, there are perennial attempts by third and fourth parties to break through the carapace of the winner-takes-all system. But its iron logic defies them, as it has an even stronger and more sustained onslaught by the Liberal Party, and latterly its Alliance, over the last three decades in Britain. The logic of the system is binary, not plural.

The binary system leads inevitably to the politics of tactical voting, squeeze or be squeezed, where, as if in an invisible French two ballot run-off system, the candidates manoeuvre to place themselves in contention in the voters' final decision. In order to reduce choice to a binary black or white decision, the negative sentiments of the voters, always and necessarily present in any election, have to be played upon and thus exaggerated. 'X is better positioned to defeat Y than is Z, so you who dislike Y more than you care for Z should vote for X.' As a result positive voting is at something of a premium in British elections.

Yet there may be an even more serious consequence of a restriction of available choice to two parties. The idea that there are only two options available to society has its roots in a revolutionary perspective. It is certainly intrinsic to Marxism and to any class-based analysis of politics that a great divide lies between the expropriators and the alienated, the bourgeoisie and the workers, which transcends all other differences in society.

It is perhaps an unrecognised victory for the Left in Britain that the modern Conservative Party, eschewing pragmatism for radical ideology, has become equally committed to the great divide:

Once to every man and nation
Comes the moment to decide
In the strife 'twixt good and evil
For the good or evil side.

So a Conservative Prime Minister now speaks of destroying socialism with a fundamentalist fervour which once belonged to the tribunes of the people.

In most modern democracies, social class and ideology are certainly two of the determinants of voting behaviour, comingled with other, regional, religious and parental affiliations but also increasingly with a more policy-based calculation of social values and personal advantage. It has been Britain's misfortune that class and ideology have bulked larger and later here than in other democracies, reinforcing in the wider society an over-adversarial system of industrial relations and a set of traditional attitudes which have impeded technological progress and economic change.

Once again it can therefore be argued that the electoral system is far from being a minor and incidental feature of the political system but that it is rather one of its main buttresses.

The question of restricted choice is related to the second claimed virtue of the present winner-take-all voting system, representation.

There is little argument in Britain with the merits of local representation, compared for instance to the national representation which smaller countries like Israel and Holland employ. Constituency elections connect the Member of Parliament to the roots of public opinion and make a reality of accountability. The advice centre or 'surgery' of a British MP, and the thousands of face-to-face meetings with constituents he will experience in the course of the year, if he is reasonably assiduous, prevent our legislators escaping completely behind the screens of nationally constructed party images.

It may be that MPs exaggerate their special local relationship and responsibility, possibly because they are deprived of any significant legislative role at Westminster. Indeed Ivor Crewe[2] has described the public perception of the MP as more an institution of last resort than a source of help. Nevertheless the constituency connection seems to be generally accepted as a genuine good in the British political culture.

Constituency representation, however, has to co-exist with a party system which is far stronger and more dynamic than the hallowed local links. The relative strength of the two elements is well illustrated by the fact that the party's candidates are chosen by relatively small groups of party members. Thus the party 'selectorate' has more say in the composition of the House of Commons than does the general electorate, particularly in the 450 safe seats, where for traditional socioeconomic reasons the result is predictable and the party's chosen candidate, once selected, is virtually sure of election.

Most voting decisions most of the time are made on party grounds. It requires an outstandingly popular or unpopular local candidate to make any significant difference to this general rule. Indeed to the extent that personality forms part of the voting decision at a General Election, it is more likely to be the personality of the party leader, whose appeal will have been tailored in a quasi-presidential way, than it is that of the local candidate.

So, an ideal British voting system would combine the principle of widespread local representation with fair party representation, and these twin considerations would affect which proportional representation system might be judged a better alternative to 'winner-takes-all'.

It would be wrong to think that the current distortion of party representation has been confined in its effects to the centre party. The Conservative Party suffers in Scotland and Wales and in the traditional Labour parts of England, with no MPs in Glasgow and Liverpool, with only 1 MP out of 6 in Sheffield despite winning one-quarter of the votes and with only 1 seat out of 15 in South Yorkshire as a whole, despite again winning one-quarter of the votes. There are no Conservative MPs, for instance, from the 100 constituencies with the highest unemployment and only 10 of the 72 MPs from Scotland are now Conservative.

By the same token, there is no longer a single Labour MP who represents an agricultural constituency, and in South-East and South-West England, with the exception of London, Labour has been virtually eliminated from representation at Westminster.

The British electoral system ensures that the notion of the 'two nations' remain a geographical and political reality and not merely a quaint historical reference. One incidental result of this polarisation, paradoxical for those who equate strong government with the winner-takes-all voting system, is that the margin of victory required in the overall popular vote to produce an overall parliamentary majority is high, a lead of 4 per cent according to Curtice and Steed.[3] Hung parliaments remain a lively statistical possibility.

This party misrepresentation is carried to an extreme in the case of the centre party, which has its vote relatively evenly distributed across the country. For the Alliance in 1987 to have secured only 3.7 per cent of the seats in return for 24.7 per cent of the votes, is so gross a distortion that it impoverishes the voter and Parliament alike. Democracy is not well served by a system where the number of seats a party wins depends less upon the votes it wins than upon the way they are distributed.

From the voter's perspective, the fact that the majority of people do not vote for a winning candidate and thus do not have 'their' MP at Westminster creates an alienation for which the co-existent idea of a local representative cannot wholly compensate. Perhaps the sporting metaphor of winners and losers is so deeply ingrained in the political culture that the majority of people do not mind being losers but the contrast with proportional representation, where most if not all the votes succeed in contributing to the election of someone who shares the voter's values, is striking.

The consequence of single-member systems is also to produce a more homogeneous and less varied type of MP than is the case in countries which use a multi-member system. The reason for this is easy to understand; in a multi-member system parties will strive for a balanced slate of candidates, appealing to various electoral interests, whereas in a single-member system a low-risk lowest common denominator candidate is more likely to be put forward. It is this which accounts for the fact that both Switzerland and Italy, countries notably less emancipated in their attitude towards female participation in public life than the United Kingdom, nevertheless have a much higher percentage of women in their legislatures than the 6.3 per cent of 41 out of 650 at Westminster.

So the British House of Commons, although unassailable in its representation of places, save perhaps for the continuing over-representation of Scotland and Wales, is deficient in personal and political representation. This deficiency is likely to lower the commitment and interest of the voters, to lessen the authority of an unrepresentative House and to deprive debates of the richness and variety of a society which is more plural in composition than its legislature.

On the other hand, an alternative PR system would surely have to retain representation of places, with an acceptable level of local proximity of the MP to the voters, if its other merits of personal and party representation are to be conceded. Both STV (the single transferable vote in multi-member constituencies) and variations of the mixed German system, like AMS (the additional member system) would do this.

The third claim of the present electoral system, and the strongest to many of its protagonists, is that, whilst it may not be in any abstract sense 'fair', it nevertheless produces strong government. This emphasis on the government-forming qualities of an election is often resisted by democratic purists concerned with the mathematical accuracy of representation – but it should not be. Elections are not only about gathering representative voices, they are also about power;

its exercise, its accountability and its peaceable transfer. When voters go to the polls it is certain that they have in the front of their minds the government they are electing and not simply the representative whom they are choosing. By the same token, the way in which election results are translated into a parliamentary pattern of government and opposition is as proper a criterion by which to judge the efficacy of an electoral system as is the mathematical fairness of the representation it produces.

However, the fact that there is more than one way of judging the efficacy of an electoral system is too often seized on by opponents of reform who, in the spirit of Isaiah Berlin pointing out that all good things are not necessarily compatible, regret the absence of fairness but claim that it is a necessary sacrifice to the greater good of strong government. A single-party majority in Parliament is so essential, it is said, that it must be conjured out of as little support as 37 per cent of those voting if necessary.

Is strong government such a considerable good that it is worth the systematic unfairness or injustice which is said to be the only way of putting it in place? Or alternatively is the whole notion of strong government a distortion of what a democratic administration should be?

After all, if 'strength' in this context means decisiveness or speed of action or ability for the executive to get its own way without argument then the strongest government, for as long as it lasts, is a dictatorship. It may be no coincidence that Lord Hailsham described the contemporary British system of government as 'elective dictatorship'. The lack of any inhibition on the executive certainly seems to have been tailor-made for strong-willed government over the past decade, since he delivered his warning.

In times of war or emergency, the democratic virtues of discussion and deliberation are naturally less valued in society than the martial strengths of resolution and salutary action. Most constitutions recognise such special times but only as exceptions to the general rules. The general rules assume that discussion and deliberation conducted in public in the legislature and freely commented upon, are not merely the necessary prelude to executive action but that they improve its quality.

In this democratic construct, the power of government is perpetually on probation, always conditional and never absolute. Does this make government less strong? Yes, it must inevitably reduce the ability of the executive to get its own way – and thus make it in one usage less strong but are there not other strengths inherent in a genuinely democratic process which enhance the real effectiveness of government?

Dictatorships are often inefficient because they do not command the consent and understanding of their subjects. A citizen democracy, by contrast, should secure a dissemination of information which increases participation, enlarges consent and promotes feedback in order to modify future decisions. Dictatorships are closed systems whereas democracies should be open to learn, changing and developing in the light of experience, looped systems.

However, our constitutional history in Britain, whilst at one level democratic, is at the same time and at a more profound level, deeply paternalistic. The Crown, and its modern successor the executive, represents a continuity of top-down authority which is stronger and more durable than modern ideas of bottom-up popular participation. The tenet, common to other democracies, that all power stems from the people is still fully not accepted in Britain. So an archaic constitution, which continues to be centred on the rights and privilege of the executive, serves to reinforce an excessive deference to the idea of strong government, and provides the perfect frame of reference for what has begun to seem in our contemporary era something very like power-worship.

Yet it must be conceded that not all advocates of strong government are worshippers of power. There are some who, whilst in every way democrats, nevertheless prefer single-party government for its clarity of direction. For them strong government may simply mean single-mindedness.

The problems with which these single-minded democrats have to wrestle are those of consent and continuity. If the votes of under 40 per cent of those voting, 30 per cent of those eligible to vote, is an adequate expression of consent for a Labour government to push through legislation giving trade unions special privileges, why should a similar level of support not be judged to be an expression of the popular will for a Conservative government to remove trade union rights? It may be that in neither case is the Government acting with the grain of public opinion as a whole but no doubt to the convinced advocate of strong government, the whole notion of acting with the grain of public opinion is itself a quibble.

For such an advocate, the function of vanguard leadership is to push ahead and to advance the frontiers, not to hang around waiting for the laggards to catch up. If a cloak of legitimacy is required for the stern joys of executive action it is found in the doctrine of the mandate, which has an air of legal weightiness to reassure any doubters. The voters are argued to have pronounced upon the incoming government's manifesto and specifically invested all its proposals with their authority.

However, even if this implausible idea of electors carefully checking off items on the parties' shopping lists bore any relation to the truth, the mandate argument would still run full tilt into the problem already discussed, that electoral victory in Britain is constructed out of a popular minority and does not rest upon the support of the majority.

Thus the sequence of British post-war government, temporarily arrested in the eighties whilst the opposition parties grapple with each other, with themselves and with the electoral system, has been of alternating minority-based governments with increasingly opposed prescriptions. Those minority-based governments have been ready to undo their predecessor's legislation and introduce contrary legislation of their own. If they feel the need to consult, it is with their parties whose unity is essential to their survival, not with the country which has had its once-and-for-all chance at the general election. The result has been discontent and discontinuity.

The alternative vision that the process of government should be incremental, each successive government building upon the achievements of its predecessors, learning from its mistakes and taking corrective action where necessary, only has to be enunciated for its naivety to be apparent in a British context. Strong government demands drastic changes in direction whilst your own capable hands are on the tiller, perhaps all the more drastic for the knowledge that sooner or later the other crew will make a 180° turn.

This raises the fourth claimed virtue of the winner-takes-all voting system; a strong opposition, fighting the government today but ready to take over when the moment comes. Yet even this rose has a worm at its heart. In our parliamentary system, is it the House of Commons as a whole which should act as a check upon the Executive? Yet if criticism is confined, as it is overwhelmingly, to the party or parties opposite, with the Government backbenchers careful to place their voices and votes at the more or less permanent disposal of the Executive, then parliamentary opposition can easily become the strident voice of faction instead of responsible constitutional review and improvement, balancing the will of the people against the imperatives of government.

Oppositions have become adversarial both in tone and policy.

Promises are made to reverse the government's measures as a matter of regular practice. Indeed the more impregnable the government's loyal majority in Parliament the more the opposition will recoil from the practical but impossible task of improving legislation now and embrace the future pleasures of promised repeal instead.

We should remind ourselves that the government's impregnable majority in Parliament will habitually have been conjured out of a minority of the votes. Yet the effect of the voting system is not to make the government proceed circumspectly, aware that it has not captured majority support, but rather the exact opposite. Differences are dramatised, the natural arrogance of governments is fortified and the understandable frustration of those who are out of power degenerates into an escapist charade, for which the price is paid when they come to power themselves, ill-prepared and over-committed.

In this clash of phantom armies, the role of the individual MP is negligible. His or her party loyalty is required and, thanks to a highly-organised system of patronage and discipline, can generally be assumed. The Select Committees, in which an MP might make a useful expert contribution or even play a pre-legislative role of forward thinking, are cruelly circumscribed compared to their counterparts abroad. Despite or perhaps because of this, it is noteworthy that these committees are the only part of the parliamentary process where a degree of bi-partisanship frequently emerges.

So, the governmental, parliamentary and electoral processes form a symbiotic relationship, each contributing to the nature of the other and fortified by it. In a spirit of constitutional experiment, it is worth considering what the effects of removing the electoral system from this interlocked relationship and replacing it by a proportional representation system might be on government and Parliament, for the effects would surely stretch far beyond the polling-booth. In particular it would mark a shift from parliamentary confrontation towards negotiation.

If it is possible to generalise about the wide variety of political systems in democratic Europe, it is in relation to one characteristic they share which profoundly differentiates them from the United Kingdom. Their systems all depend upon negotiation rather than confrontation between parties. By extension this negotiation process which permeates their legislatures often seems to stretch out to include relationships between interest-groups, business and trade unions, or between the centre of government and the localities. This system of negotiation politics has also become the practice of the

European Community, to the frequent and apparent mystification of the British. In the United States, without proportional representation or a multi-party system, a similar process of mutual accommodation is reached through the trade-offs required by the separation of powers.

Britain looks increasingly isolated in the way it legitimises the exercise of unlimited central power by whichever minority party is successful in grasping the apparatus of the state and sustaining its manufactured majority in Parliament.

Proportional representation would mean one of two things for the British parties if they wished to form a government: either they would have to reach out substantially beyond their traditional class and regional strongholds for the support of the majority of the voters and inevitably in the process re-direct their appeal from the ideological minority of partisans to the more pragmatic centre-ground; or, more probably, even if they behaved in this way, as the voting system would reward them for doing, but nevertheless failed in getting 50 per cent of the votes or more, they would have to negotiate with other parties to find a common-ground of agreement. In either event, the consequences would be momentous for the parties themselves and for the political system of which they are the custodians and operators.

Manifestos would become statements of intention, the starting point for discussion, rather than being fixed prescriptions. Parties would have to keep their eyes and ears attuned more keenly to the wishes of the electorate and less to those of the faithful partisans. Politicians would have to develop the neglected arts of conciliation and consensus and throw away at least some of the armour of self-righteousness. Parliament might even become more of a forum and less of a battlefield, with the government obliged to inform and persuade in its search for majority consent.

It may be objected that such fundamental changes would require not only an institutional but also a cultural change in the political process. No doubt they would, and one which those habituated to the present systems of Westminster and Whitehall would find difficult to accept. Yet change is already pressing in from the European Community and the culture of indivisible sovereign power is subtly shifting towards one of pluralistic accommodation. Electoral reform may well be the prerequisite for this shift to gather momentum and a new culture of negotiation to emerge.

Electoral reform would also redefine relationships between the parties in a way which would make them more consistent with the values of contemporary society. Choice, and the engine of competition which drives it, are now generally accepted across the political spectrum as being to the benefit of the consumer, enlarging personal expression and opportunity. At the same time there is also a general sense that to maintain competition, and thereby to promote genuine choice, markets cannot be left entirely to themselves or they may become conspiracies against the consumer whom they purport to serve. Should some of this thinking not be applied in the sphere of political choice, the democratic system, as well as in the sphere of choice of products and services, the economy?

Parties can and should compete with each other for the first preference of the elector. In some areas of policy no doubt this will mean they will resemble each other, particularly where there is a very wide acceptance of certain values in society at large. In other areas they may be sharply differentiated, competing for contrasting agendas and views of society or even of human nature itself. They will be performing their proper function of organising public choice.

But electoral reform and a switch to a system of proportional representation, could help to ensure that, just as in a properly regulated marketplace, the playing-field of competition was level. The present duopoly, which has some of the characteristics of a market-sharing cartel, would not be acceptable. Parties would have to be ready and willing to face the bracing winds of genuine competition.

Even more profoundly they would have to accept each others' right to exist and the validity of each others' viewpoint, albeit continuing to believe in and assert their own superior merit. Other parties would be their competitors not their enemies, to be beaten not destroyed. Mutual acceptance of competitive diversity is a necessary condition of democratic pluralism. Only millenarians, looking for the permanent victory of their revolutionary cause, believe otherwise.

Electoral reform would make British party politics more of a process of competitive co-existence and less of a destructive end-game. Today's rival might in certain circumstances be tomorrow's ally and greater care would therefore have to be taken before extreme language or exaggeration of difference was deployed. Competition would both be sharpened by equality of treatment at the polls and yet regulated within the bounds of the general will and a negotiated exercise of power.

To some this vision of a reformed political system may seem tame, lacking the drama of confrontation and the unswerving conviction of those who believe they fight the good fight. To others who have observed the way in which the rising tide of partisanship has filled the vacuum at the heart of the constitution, some change in the nature and direction of the parties, who are themselves the source of that partisanship, would be welcome. A system, based on proportional representation, which enforced on the parties the necessity of both competing and cooperating with each other might bring them closer to the reality of the same inescapable and proper tension between those two poles of competition and cooperation which exists in individual and social life and which is the source of progress. In that and other senses a change to proportional representation in Britain should properly be considered a question of the first constitutional significance.

Notes

1. John Stuart Mill, *On Liberty*, Blackwell, Oxford, 1946.
2. Ivor Crewe, in Vernon Bogdanor (ed.), *Representatives of the People?*, Gower, London, 1985.
3. Curtice and Steed, Butler and Kavanagh, *Nuffield Election Study 1987*, Macmillan, London, 1987.

9 Official Secrecy and Freedom of Information

James Cornford

> Knowledge is power. It is important to recognise that the issue of open government is about power, political power, a shift in power, its redistribution. The government of the United Kingdom has in its possession a vast store of information and the ability to withhold information and to judge the timing of its publication is a part of political power. Open government entails increasing publication of official information to the press and the public who, with the power given by greater knowledge of the activities of government, are better able to assess, criticise and bring pressure to bear on the government's performance. It is essentially a political issue.
>
> Lord Franks[1]

The law relating to official information is unsatisfactory whether it be in respect of the protection of official secrets and government confidentiality, of legitimate public access to official information, of the safeguarding of personal privacy, or of the maintenance of an efficient system of official record-keeping and a proper national archive. These matters – protection, access, privacy and records – are closely related and proposals for reform in the law relating to any one of them must take the others into account. In an ideal world one would plan a coherent reform embracing them all. There is no prospect of a grand design: progress will be piecemeal if it takes place at all and the best we can hope for is to strive for consistency and to avoid the pitfalls marked out by other countries where incompatible provisions have been enacted. Concern about access to personal information and protection against its misuse is probably the major cause for public anxiety about official information in this country, the main reason for support for Freedom of Information legislation, and the subject of the largest proportion of requests for access under such legislation overseas.

An important advance has already been made in this field with the Data Protection Act 1984. This does not, however, extend to information not held in machine-readable form; there are distinct limitations on access to personal files held in both the public and private sectors; and it is not yet clear how far the Act can be made to work at all. The principles are fine but their wide application makes it doubtful that the Registrar will be able to make the Act effective. But at least any proposals for public rights of access to official information should not conflict with the principles of data protection: the aim should be to extend them to all forms of personal records. This was attempted by Archy Kirkwood's *Access to Personal Files Act* (1987), but his Bill was emasculated by the government and most personal files not held on computer whether in the public or the private sector remain closed. Access to personal files is only one aspect of privacy, which raises more general questions connected to a Bill of Rights and the European Convention which are treated elsewhere.

Protection, access and public records have to be considered together first because the questions as to what official information ought to be kept secret (and protected by criminal sanctions), what confidential and what available to the public need to be dealt with together; and second because the Public Records Act 1967 provides a right of public access subject to certain important limitations. Rights of access to official information before and after it is transferred to the Public Record Office must be coherently related.

I want to look in some detail at current proposals for reform: Mr Richard Shepherd's Bill on Section 2 of the Official Secrets Act, the latest version of the Freedom of Information Bill introduced by Mr David Steel in 1984, and the less exciting but critical question of how access might be made to work in practice. I make no apologies for this. Many people recognise that the present law is a mess. Fewer understand exactly what is wrong. And fewer still know in any detail what is proposed in its place. The detail is important; many doubts about reform can only be met by drawing attention to what is actually proposed. But there is a prior question of political judgement, even of faith or temperament. Should there be a statutory right of access to official information or are we content for disclosure to remain entirely within the discretion of government? Some proponents of greater openness in government believe that it can be achieved by executive discretion (the view of successive governments) and some by an extension of the concept of maladministration to govern certain refusals of information under a code enforced by the Parliamentary Commissioner.[2] I do not believe that a major shift in the balance between government and the public will be achieved without a statutory right. There are many practical difficulties in the proposal, and the right will not be as extensive or revolutionary as enthusiastic supporters hope. Nevertheless the establishment of such a right would make a decisive change in the assumptions upon which government is conducted and in the long run disperse the pervasive ethos of secrecy. I take the notion of Elective Dictatorship seriously. The present law is certainly consonant with our constitutional tradition: the question is whether the power granted to the Executive is something we want to preserve.

The dependence of the Executive on Parliament is fundamental: parliamentary questions, select committees and the ultimate deterrent of votes of confidence serve to hold governments to account and to limit their freedom of action. But given the extent of prerogative powers derived from the Crown, the effective control of the procedures of Parliament, the mastery of the civil service, and the ability to manipulate and bully the media, there need to be some countervailing measures to shift the balance towards Parliament and the public. If this involves constitutional change, so be it. Whatever the historical origins of the constitution, the legitimacy of today's governments rests on the informed consent of the people. The hallowed doctrine of ministerial responsibility, called in aid whenever there is an attempt to limit the powers of government, is less than convincing when ministers can determine whether those to whom they are accountable know enough to hold them to account. I do not mean to suggest that governments are in truth all-powerful. There is a great contrast between their formidable advantages over their critics and their inability to deal with the many intractable problems which confront them. Perhaps this explains the sterility of constitutional debate.

PROTECTION

The saga of Section 2 of the Official Secrets Act 1911 is too familiar to bear much repetition. Suffice it to say that some statutory backing for the duty of confidentiality of public servants is necessary; that Section 2 has provided it; that the prosecutions brought under it have not been frequent and that the majority have been successful and uncontroversial. But Section 2 has been used to cover a multitude of sins: from corrupt use of official information for personal gain, to ex-servicemen talking to journalists about their experiences, to civil servants leaking documents which show their masters in a bad light.

Over the last twenty years the indiscriminate nature of the offences created by Section 2 has led to a number of unsuccessful prosecutions in which the government's case has collapsed, the presiding judge has criticised the law or the jury has returned a perverse verdict rather than enforce it. From the government's point of view, the law has become, if not inoperable, certainly unreliable. All this has been recognised for twenty years or more. Section 2 was examined and found wanting by a committee under the chairmanship of Lord Franks,[3] whose recommendations were accepted by successive governments and finally emerged with significant modifications in the Protection of Official Information Bill, 1979.[4]

The problem with Section 2 is that it protects all information, no matter how trivial. It creates absolute offences without regard to the intentions of the offender or the damage caused by the offence. It creates the offence of 'unauthorised disclosure' without giving any indication of who can authorise whom to disclose what, and the offences include the disclosure or receipt of information which is already publicly available. It introduces furthermore the concept of 'the interests of the state' which is alien to our constitutional usage and a sore puzzle to the judges who have had to interpret it. The Franks Report argued that the best solution was to start again: to uncouple the protection of confidentiality from the punishment of espionage and sabotage with which it is linked in Section 2; to limit the information covered to that which warrants the imposition of criminal sanctions, rather than disciplinary measures; to define the offences in terms of intention and effect; and to link the question of damage to the definition of the information to be protected by means of the security classification given to official papers. The last point is important because it would provide civil servants with an immediate and fairly reliable guide to the kind of information they are handling. The Government's 1979 Bill followed the Franks' prescription in most respects, but it differed in the range of information to be protected; it did not link the test of damage (serious injury to the interests of the nation) to the procedures for classification; it did not apply any test to information relating to security and intelligence; and the defence of prior publication was limited to information supplied to the government in confidence by individuals and other bodies.

The press in particular took strong exception to this Bill, which it regarded as likely to be more effective than the discredited Section 2 and equally obnoxious. Whether this would have been enough to cause its withdrawal is doubtful. But the introduction of the Bill happened to coincide with the revelations about Sir Anthony Blunt, renewed controversy about the security services and demands for inquiries and parliamentary scrutiny. The Government withdrew the Bill and there matters rested until 1987, when Mr Richard Shepherd MP came top of the private members' ballot and decided to introduce a new Protection of Official Information Bill, closely modelled on Franks and the 1979 Bill. On this occasion the Government proved more resolute and took the unprecedented step of issuing a three-line whip to defeat Mr Shepherd's Bill at second reading. There was a lively and entertaining debate which, however, leaves us guessing as to the nature of the government's objections. The Home Secretary's remarks were confined to stressing the urgency of the matter, its complexity, his unreadiness to comment on matters of substance, and his promise to introduce a White Paper in June 1988 and a Bill in the following session.[5] But it is not too hard to guess where the Government may have difficulties with Mr Shepherd's Bill. The first and perhaps least important concerns the scope of information to be protected. Both the 1979 Bill and Mr Shepherd's Bill cover information concerning defence, foreign relations, security and intelligence, and law enforcement. The 1979 Bill includes also information given in confidence both by individuals and by corporate bodies. Mr Shepherd does not include information from corporate bodies because: 'to do so would be to protect a vast amount of information on subjects such as nuclear and environmental pollution, food additives, pesticides, pharmaceuticals and consumer product safety. The fact that such information is covered by Section 2 of the Official Secrets Act 1911 is one reason why there is general resentment and much disquiet about Section 2. Certainly, some civil servants handle commercially sensitive information obtained from private concerns, but so too do local authority officials who have never been subject to Section 2. Should an official improperly disclose a company's trade secrets, no doubt he or she would be open to an action for recovery of damages under common law, which might involve potentially enormous personal liability'.[6] One may doubt that the Government's corporate clients, public or private, will be happy with this. They ought to be made to accept it, however, since asking for information in confidence is the classic device for excluding the public from knowledge of what is being done in their name and for their benefit, in such matters as pollution control and safety at work.

The second and much more sensitive matter is that Mr Shepherd has gone back to Franks and applied the test of serious injury to the interests of the nation in any prosecution for the unauthorised disclosure of information relating to defence, international relations, *security or intelligence.* In its 1979 Bill the Government proposed that there should be no such test for information relating to security or intelligence. This position is consistent with the Government's present line on the absolute duty of lifelong confidentiality for anyone who has worked in the security services. Mr Shepherd does not believe that people should be sent to prison, as opposed to being sacked or disciplined, unless their actions have done serious damage. The official view is that any disclosure relating to security is potentially damaging and that it is impossible for outsiders to know whether or not the damage is serious and a potential threat to security to have to prove that it is.[7] The impression given in the debate on Mr Shepherd's Bill is that parliamentary confidence in the performance of the security services is not high and that blanket-protection will not be readily conceded, unless in return for some form of parliamentary scrutiny.

Mr Shepherd's Bill also returns to Franks in linking the test of serious injury to classification, but with this important difference: Franks recommended that the minister's certificate to the effect that information was properly classified at the time of the alleged offence should be final. There could therefore be no argument as to the damage caused by an unauthorised disclosure. Mr Shepherd, mindful perhaps of the tendency of ministers to confuse embarrassment to themselves with serious injury to the interests of the nation, as witnessed in the cases of Miss Tisdall and Mr Ponting, provided for a review of the ministerial certificate by the Judicial Committee of the Privy Council, before the trial proper. This is a compromise between ministerial fiat and full justiciability, but it has at least the merit that it should cause ministers and the Attorney-General to think carefully before launching a prosecution. This is certainly a proposal which will cause problems for the Government. But the dangers of overclassification and the failure to declassify information that has become less sensitive with time are obvious. Mr Jonathan Aitken, MP, one of the sponsors of Mr Shepherd's Bill, spoke forcefully from his own experience of the need to be able to challenge the ministerial certificate. At his own trial for an alleged offence under Section 2: 'The Crown opened its case in dramatic terms saying that "major military secrets" had been revealed. That statement was made by the prosecutors on, of course, the submission by Ministers.

Two days later, after some cross-examination of the chief prosecution witnesses, it was revealed that every military fact in the document concerned had already been published and that the British defence attaché, whose document had been leaked, had himself read out the document to a press conference of journalists on an unattributable basis. Halfway through the trial, therefore, the Crown had to go into reverse and say, "very sorry. There are actually no secrets here." If Ministers' decisions cannot be reviewed, a future defendant might be unable to argue about the assertion that secrets had been revealed.'[8]

This brings us naturally to the third point at which Mr Shepherd has parted company with the 1979 Bill, namely the defence of prior publication. In the 1979 Bill the defence that information was already publicly available applied only to information supplied in confidence by individuals or other bodies. Mr Shepherd extended this defence to cover all forms of information. In the light of its travails with *Spycatcher*, it is not difficult to see why the government may find this a hard pill to swallow. Again the argument will come back to the question of damage: if the offence is to be judged by the extent of the damage done, the security services will argue that the publication of any information about them is likely to be damaging, no matter how trivial it may appear to be. Each separate piece of information may be harmless by itself, but brought together they form a jigsaw puzzle which can only prove helpful to those whom it is the duty of the security services to keep under surveillance. This is quite properly special pleading and will be for the Government to convince a sceptical parliament that there is a special case.

Finally, and perhaps most contentiously, Mr Shepherd has provided a public-interest defence for those accused of unauthorised disclosure. Clause 7(1) of his Bill runs as follows:

> It shall be a defence for a person charged under this Act to prove that the disclosure or retention of the information or article was in the public interest insofar as he had reasonable cause to believe that it indicated the existence of crime, fraud, abuse of authority, neglect in the performance of an official duty or other misconduct.

Under clause 7(2) this defence would only be available to a crown servant or government contractor if he had taken 'reasonable steps to comply with any established procedures for drawing such misconduct to the attention of the appropriate authorities without effect'.

In introducing the Bill Mr Shepherd had the following to say of this provision:

> The principle of a public interest defence is, of course, not new. It is taken from the existing common law of confidence which has long held that a person cannot be bound to respect an obligation of confidentiality to conceal serious wrongdoing. In a 1968 judgement, Lord Denning held that the defence 'extends to any misconduct of such a nature that it ought in the public interest to be disclosed to others'. He went on to say: 'It should extend to crimes, frauds and misdeeds, both those actually committed as well as those in contemplation, provided always – this is essential – that the disclosure is justified in the public interest.'[9]

The defence is in fact a much more limited one than the name may imply. If such a defence were successful in a particular case the accused involved would escape penalties of up to two years imprisonment and a fine. A successful defence to a criminal prosecution would not necessarily mean that the accused would retain or regain a job as a crown servant or otherwise. That would involve a separate decision by the employer, which would be reviewed (if at all: crown servants, strictly speaking, have no contract of employment) by an industrial tribunal. It is a defence of last resort for an action of last resort which no civil servant would lightly undertake.

Nor is it a proposal which the Government will take lightly, since it touches both on the sensitive nerve of the relations between ministers and civil servants and on the equally sensitive problem of who is to define the public interest. The defence is based on the analogy with the law of confidence that there can be no confidence in iniquity. But following Lord Denning it will not be enough to argue that wrongdoing has occured. The wrongdoing will have to be of such gravity that it justifies the disclosure of information that would otherwise be properly protected for reasons of national security or law enforcement or privacy. And this takes us back to a problem earlier referred to: how is the court to determine what the public interest is? The problem is not whether the public interest or the interests of the state are synonymous with the interests of the government of the day. They cannot be. Ministers may wish to exceed their powers or to commit other illegal acts. The support of Parliament, save in the form of legislation, cannot make such actions constitutional or legal. Civil servants are bound not to obey illegal orders and indeed may be bound to fulfil statutory obligations whether ministers like it or not.[10] The problem remains of who is to say what the interests of the State are. The judges faced with this conundrum in the Chandler and Ponting cases, lacking clear statutory guidance and any constitutional document, have fallen back on the argument that the Government alone can define what the public, national or state interest is: no other body has the authority to do so. The judges cannot do it themselves and nobody in Whitehall or Westminster wants them to. Nor will there be much enthusiasm for leaving the matter to a jury. But if there is not to be even this limited defence for conscientiously-disturbed civil servants, they will have to be given something better than the last resort offered in Lord Armstrong's note of guidance: 'if the matter (about which the civil servant is disturbed) still cannot be resolved on a basis which the civil servant concerned is able to accept, he or she must either carry out his or her instructions or resign from the public service – though even after resignation he or she will still be bound to keep the confidences to which he or she has become privy as a civil servant'.[11] Obedience, resignation and silence: what a prospect for a civil servant who believes that his minister is deliberately misleading Parliament or conniving at some more palpable wrongdoing. I hope I have said enough to show that there are likely to be serious differences between Mr Shepherd's Bill and whatever the Home Secretary eventually unveils. But this should not obscure the fact that there are major areas of agreement and that by building on the foundations laid by Franks, a reform by Section 2 acceptable to a wide spread of opinion could be achieved without enormous difficulty. The same cannot be said about public rights of access to official information.

ACCESS

Reform of Section 2 will not of itself increase freedom of information: there may be some relaxation in respect of information no longer protected by criminal sanctions, but civil servants will be under the same duty of confidentiality, sustained by their own professional standards and by disciplinary regulations. Ministers may be more open, as they have been; but they need not be so and the advantages of controlling the flow of information and the timing of disclosure will remain. I do not want to repeat here the general argument for a right of public access but to describe what it involves and how it might be made to work. The general principles have been set out in a recommendation of the Committee of Ministers of the Council of Europe to the member states as follows:

(i) Everyone within the jurisdiction of a member state shall have a right to obtain, on request, information held by the public authorities other than legislative bodies and judicial authorities.
(ii) Effective and appropriate means shall be provided to ensure access to information.
(iii) Access to information shall not be refused on the ground that the requesting person does not have a specific interest in the matter.
(iv) Access to information shall be provided on the basis of equality.
(v) The foregoing principles shall apply subject only to such limitations and restrictions as are necessary in a democratic society (such as national security, public safety, the prevention of crime or for preventing the disclosure of information received in confidence) and for the protection of privacy and other legitimate interests, having, however, due regard to the specific interest of an individual in information held by the public authorities which concerns him personally.
(vi) Any request for information shall be decided upon within a reasonable time.
(vii) A public authority refusing access to information shall give the reasons on which the refusal is based, according to law and practice.
(viii) Any refusal of information shall be subject to review on request.[12]

The Freedom of Information (No. 2) Bill, 1984 represents the third or fourth attempt to put these principles into statutory form in a way compatible with the constitutional and administrative arrangements of the United Kingdom.[13] Thus the Bill proposes a right of access for all members of the public without any requirement to state a reason for requiring access. This is the cardinal principle of Freedom of Information: the onus is shifted from the citizen having to show cause for wanting information to the Government for wanting to withhold it. It follows from this that no purpose is served by trying to limit the classes of person to whom access must be granted. It would always be possible for those denied access to get it by proxy. The right of access is to all documents held by government departments and authorities (listed in a schedule) save for documents containing 'exempt information'. 'Document' is broadly defined but the important point is that access is to information in the form in which the department actually holds it. There is no right created to subject departments to inquisition. The definition of a document is in itself a problem: does it refer to the formal record of departmental work: agreed minutes, official correspondence and so forth; or does it include the working papers and preparatory notes of civil servants? Practice abroad differs. The broader definition is more revealing, more troublesome and more expensive. It is also what most advocates of Freedom of Information in Britain want. It touches on a raw constitutional nerve and threatens the traditional conception of the relations between ministers and civil servants. The Freedom of Information (No. 2) Bill has recognised the problem and provided an exemption for policy advice of which more below. This may be a disappointment to some, but I do not believe that it is ever going to be possible to get at the inside story of policymaking as it unfolds.[14] But access to formal records of departmental and interdepartmental committees and correspondence, to internal reports, technical appraisals and forecasts, would certainly alter the balance of advantage between departments and their critics, and between ministers and Parliament, and expose the executive to much more searching scrutiny after and nearer the event.

Access need not be given to documents containing exempt information and in some cases must not be given. Exemptions can be defined in a variety of ways, including the exemption of specific documents, as is the practice in Sweden, and the exclusion of whole departments or subject areas from the right of access. Since exemption is likely to be the main battleground over the extent of freedom of information, it is important that exemptions be defined in such a way that the reason for refusing access should be part of the definition, so that there is an opportunity to contest refusals of access. The exemptions in the Freedom of Information (No. 2) Bill are drawn up on this basis. There can clearly be argument about the scope of the exemptions. Those relating to commercial confidentiality and to policy advice raise particular problems, of which more below. The essential point, however, is that each exemption should be based on a reason – a threat to military security, impeding law enforcement, invading privacy and so forth – rather than a category of document. The government must give reasons why in the public interest information should be withheld.

The exemption on grounds of commercial confidentiality presents problems, first because there is a legitimate public interest in having access to much information supplied to government by business and second because weak exemptions, such as those in the US Freedom of Information Act, are alleged to have provided a field day for a form of licensed industrial espionage and have given rise to much litigation.[15] There is a difficult balance to be achieved and an added complication to the resolution of disputes over access. The exemption proposed in the Freedom of Information (No. 2) Bill relates to financial, commercial, scientific and technical information and has two parts. The first refers to information which is *required* to be given to a department 'the disclosure of which would give an unfair advantage to the competitors of the party concerned'. And the second refers to information obtained in confidence without statutory powers and not in return for any grant or benefit 'the disclosure of which would impair the ability of the department or authority to obtain similar information in the future'. The first definition does not prevent disclosures which might harm a business in its dealings with suppliers or contractors and probably needs to be modified. The exemption has, however, been deliberately drawn to avoid using as the main criterion whether or not disclosure would result in financial loss. Many disclosures which ought to be permitted may well, as a side-effect, lead to financial loss. The revelation, for instance, that a company's products were dangerous may well lead to losses if customers decide to buy safer competing products as a result. This would give competitors an advantage – but a fair rather than unfair one.

The exemption may also allow the disclosure of information about products that is known to competitors, but concealed from customers. For example, information about the composition of products may be kept from customers to give the impression that they are buying a unique product made to a secret formula, when in fact the product may be identical to many on the market. The secrecy merely prevents the customer from realising that the same thing can be bought more cheaply elsewhere. Disclosure of such information would be in line with recent legislation requiring foods, medicines and products containing hazardous chemicals to have labels showing their composition. Finally, third-party information which is potentially exempt could be released where there is a public interest in its disclosure, to protect public health for example, if this clearly outweighed the commercial interests involved. The second provision would allow departments to withhold certain information if disclosure would impair their ability to obtain such information from third parties in future. The exemption could only be invoked if the department had no statutory power to demand that the information be supplied and the information was not supplied in return for a direct benefit. Again there is a balance to be struck between the public interest in departments securing information beyond that which they can require and the public interest in allowing access to it. It is next to impossible to legislate for such cases and much will inevitably be left to negotiation and bargaining as well as the arbitration of the Information Commissioner whose role is described below.

The other exemption which is both important and contentious is that governing policy advice. Earlier versions of the Bill exempted Cabinet papers as such and policy papers for a limited period. But it soon became apparent that few people directly involved in government thought this went far enough to protect the confidential relationship between ministers and civil servants. The exemption now permits withholding of any information which would disclose anything in the nature of 'opinion or advice or recommendation tended by any person in the course of his official duties for the purpose of the formation of policy within a department or authority'. Excluded from this definition of policy advice are factual information, expert opinion on a technical issue or on the interpretation of data or the reports of any advisory committee established as a discrete body. Are these practicable distinctions or will this exemption provide an excuse to withhold all documents bearing on policy, because it proves impossible to separate fact from advice? For once there is some native evidence to help us. In 1977 the then head of the Civil Service Sir Douglas Allen, now Lord Croham, issued a directive to Permanent Secretaries telling them to produce factual and analytical material used in policymaking in such a way as to be easily separable from the advice based on that material. The factual information was to be made available to the public.

The effect of the Croham directive was monitored by *The Times* and assessed by Colin Bennett and Peter Hennessy for the Outer Circle Policy Unit.[16] They found that the release of background information on which internal policy decision were based came in a variety of forms: external or internal committee or working party reports, consultative documents, statistical calculations and transcripts of conferences. They observed that some departments did better than others. In some cases documents even bore the names of individual civil servants. One important feature of the Croham directive was that it told departments that 'henceforth the working assumption should be that such (background) material will be published unless they decide it should not be' and that 'therefore when policy studies are being undertaken in future the background material should as far as possible be written in a form which would permit it to be published separately with the minimum of alteration'. This approach marked an important shift from the doctrine inculcated through the Official Secrets Acts that all information should be considered secret unless somebody authorised its publication.

The initiatives undertaken as a result of the Croham directive petered out with the change of government in 1979. But the exercise demonstrated three things: that factual information can be separated from policy advice; that civil servants were prepared to publish information voluntarily; and most importantly that without a continuing will to publish information, voluntary arrangements can easily be changed.

The exemptions in the Freedom of Information (No. 2) Bill are broad: they are deliberately designed to provide a basis for questioning a department's claims to withhold information. Some mechanism will be required to resolve disputes between departments and applicants over their interpretation. What is proposed in the Bill in the first instance is an Information Commissioner, a hybrid of the Parliamentary Commissioner for Administration, the Data Protection Registrar and the Canadian FOI Commissioner. The Commissioner is required to investigate complaints about refusals of access and other matters such as unreasonable delay. He also has powers to initiate investigations and to command witnesses and papers. Where he finds a complaint justified, he must make an order requiring the department to grant access or take other specified action, subject to appeal to the Tribunal. The Commissioner's role is similar to that of the Parliamentary Commissioner but his powers of investigation are more extensive. These are drawn from the provisions of the Canadian Act. In addition he has the power subject to the Tribunal to order the disclosure or correction of a document.

The Tribunal is modelled on the Data Protection Tribunal, though in the FOI Bill both departments and individuals may appeal to the Tribunal from the decisions of the Commissioner. There are two exemptions which are likely to give rise to particular difficulties, judging by experience in the United States. These are the exemptions for commercial confidences and for privacy. Provision has therefore been made to allow third parties affected by the granting of access to information provided by or about them to be notified of and to be allowed to appeal to the Tribunal against the granting of access.

These proposals are based on the assumption that the greater part of the work of policing the exemptions will involve investigations similar to those undertaken by the Parliamentary Commissioner for Administration, but that if the Act is to have teeth he needs greater powers of investigation and the ability to order disclosure. The composition and procedures of the Tribunal are drawn from the Data Protection Act with powers derived from the Canadian FOI Act. Tribunal proceedings would be in public except where they concern exempt information. Since any question of access will almost certainly involve disputes about exemptions it is likely that a large part of the Tribunal's work will involve *ex parte* representation and hearings and deliberations *in camera*. Cases involving obstruction, delay or the correction of documents would not raise the same problems, but the Commissioner ought to be able to sort out most complaints of that kind.

The major complication of the procedures for granting access, which affects Commissioner and Tribunal alike, is the provision for the notification and participation of third parties affected by the disclosure of information which may fall under the exemptions for commercial confidentiality and privacy. It is clearly important to make provision of this kind: access to commercial information is bound to be especially contentious. There is no obvious way of doing this without a notification procedure which inevitably adds to delay. The length of the appeals procedure suggests that the Tribunal will be important in setting precedents rather than in resolving particular disputes. The Commissioner may establish a more informal relationship with departments which will enable him to help resolve the problems of applicants without resort to formal investigation or appeal.

I dwell on these hypothetical arrangements to illustrate the problems of access and the improvisation required to offer plausible solutions to them. There is necessarily a degree of borrowing from what look to be the most satisfactory and appropriate provisions in existing Freedom of Information Acts. There is no one model that can be transferred whole: we cannot copy Sweden or the United States or even Australia or Canada and indeed do not want to: hence the spare parts surgery. But we can learn from their experience and their mistakes. Many of the issues are ones which call for political judgement and there can be wide differences of view between those who support a public right of access.

In the last part of this paper I want to look at the practical problems of making access possible, which involves the recognition of certain ineluctable facts about the present nature of public records and some speculation about the possibilities for the future which are perhaps more radical than anything proposed so far.[17] The Freedom of Information (No. 2) Bill envisages a system in which anyone applying for access must normally specify the document he wants to see. Departments are therefore required to provide publicly available indexes to the documents they hold and to publish Codes of Guidance describing how members of the public may apply for, inspect, copy and correct documents. Departments must reply to requests for access within 30 days. Where access is granted the document must be made available for inspection and copying as soon as is practicable. Where access is refused, departments must give reasons in writing and inform the applicant of his right to complain to the Information Commissioner and subsequently to apply for review to the Information Tribunal. All very neat: but these provisions raise a great many practical questions, not least the ability of Whitehall departments to locate and index the documents in their possession.

RECORDS

Access can only be made to work if applicants can find out what is in departmental records and if documents can be located and copied quickly and without great expense: the problems here are (a) the bulk of department files: shelf-mile after shelf-mile; (b) departmental practices: files contain several documents and are organised for the working requirements of departments; it would be difficult to index them in their present state; (c) weeding: departments destroy a large proportion of their records before they are transferred to the Public Records Office. Departments destroy on administrative grounds, which may not coincide with either the short- or long-term interests of potential outside users. The PRO could not conceivably preserve all these documents even if it wanted to. Weeding takes place after consultation, but the considerations applied by PRO are necessarily different from those of FOI.[18]

There is therefore a strong case for saying that any legislation for access cannot be retrospective for practical reasons: it will require new methods of handling documents in departments which they will require notice to develop. It must, however, be noted that the

Australians and Canadians have not experienced insuperable difficulties with retrospective access and, as with many of the practical problems of FOI, there is a tendency to exaggerate the difficulties for essentially political reasons. It should be possible to provide for retrospective access subject to certain conditions, such as a longer period allowed to departments to respond to requests, or additional exemptions for documents which are particularly hard to locate. At the least, retrospective access should be possible to certain classes of documents, such as those relating to individuals, which generate most requests and are also most easily identified.

CHARACTERISTICS OF THE PRESENT SYSTEM

The present system puts the control of official information completely within the discretion of government, with the limited exception of the rights of public access established by the Public Records Acts, 1958 and 1967. The main characteristics of this discretionary system are:

(i) Official information is organised for the purpose of policymaking and administration on a departmental basis with little consultation or oversight;

(ii) When records have ceased to be required for these purposes there is a phased transfer to the PRO after review and selection in departments: the main criteria for preservation are administrative; there are variable rights of access, subject to exceptions and discretion, which are not subject to any effective independent scrutiny.

(iii) Apart from the transfer of records to the PRO, the publication and release of information takes place at the instance and for the purposes of government, in specially prepared form, subject to the political interest of governments and their relations with the suppliers of information.

There are three major problems with this system:

(1) The efficiency of the system for the purposes of government and administration itself: departmental systems of filing may make retrieval or cross-referencing difficult or impossible. Departments mislay, overlook or simply are ignorant of information in their possession.[19]

(2) The destruction of records which ought to be kept for historical

reasons, either on political grounds or from failure to appreciate their significance: departments generally give the work of selection a low priority and the quality of the work leaves much to be desired. The recommendations of the Grigg Report for review procedures in departments have been changed in effect from the notion that if any record is needed administratively it should be preserved whether needed historically or not, to the practice that if a record is not needed administratively it is destroyed whether needed historically or not.[20]

(3) The quality and value of the information released: what is released at the behest of government may not be released in the form most useful to outside users, either because of timing, partial disclosure or political bias in the presentation of information.

It is the third of these reasons which has led to the demand for FOI, but the establishment of a public right of access would also provide the opportunity for a reform of public records-keeping which would make it more flexible and efficient both for immediate governmental purposes and for longer-term historical uses. Where FOI has been imposed on an existing system and caused dislocation and enormous expense, one long-term effect has been to improve methods of record-keeping. In the light of, say, the experience in the United States, we can anticipate these problems, both by avoiding retrospective legislation and by reorganising public record-keeping in a system which is equally compatible for purposes of administration, access and preservation.[21]

What is proposed is that public access, departmental use and archival requirements should be handled as a single system of record management. This looks a tall order but it should be emphasised that nothing which is being proposed here is new and untried: the following proposals are an amalgam of practices now being put into effect successfully by many organisations and by government departments in other countries. There will undoubtedly be difficulties and costs associated with a change of system on this scale, but it may be of some comfort to know that many of the difficulties have already been overcome on a smaller scale and that some of the costs have been compensated for by increased efficiency in the handling of information. If the political case for FOI has been established, then the problem is to work out the most advantageous means of putting it into effect.

One possibility would be to create a single service covering the different requirements of the various government departments as well as those outside. A single system would have to be designed with certain checks and barriers to limit both internal and external access to certain categories of information, especially personal information held by the Home Office, Inland Revenue and DHSS. It would also require agreement that it was both feasible and desirable on administrative grounds. In view of the variety of departmental interests, the strength of their traditions, constitutional considerations and the limitations on the transfer of information between departments on grounds of security, privacy and confidentiality, the adoption of a common system is unlikely and probably undesirable.

The alternative is to provide common guidelines for the adoption of individually-tailored systems with provision for limited cooperation between departments. Such systems will require the amalgamation of various units handling information within each department, viz. the department library, registry and information office. The library may well prove the best focus for the new scheme, since the new system will be more akin to library work, already familiar with multiple users and multiple access, than to that of the traditional departmental registry, whose clientele are usually those creating and using a limited number of files on a continuing basis. Most requests to a registry are by file classification number or short title and relate to a specific administrative function or responsibility which is clearly definable. The users are normally familiar with the file classification system or that part they use regularly.

Public Access (and privacy) legislation produces new clients, whose requests are related to a subject rather than to a specific departmental activity or record, so that it is necessary to be able to identify the information wherever it is located in departmental records, and usually at short notice. Since there may well be resistance among senior administrators to radical changes in their working practices, it should be emphasised that it would be perfectly feasible to retain a registry with its manual files organised on the old basis, as long as all information is also fed into the new system. This dual system would be retained until a new generation of administrators familiar with computer terminals, word processors, VDUs and so forth reaches the top (in ten years perhaps?).

Departments may need to continue old and new systems for an extended period of transition. One possibility would be the installation of stand-alone systems (compatible with existing departmental systems) which would be the first stage in a progression which would eventually lead to computer integration trials of stand-alone systems (word processors) and which have in fact already taken place in government departments.[22] During the transition period it may be difficult to justify the cost-effectiveness of the programme, but developments in management information services already underway indicate that effective programmes exist and that implementation of the proposals outlined here would be relatively easy. Examples are the English Health Services Information Group, and the development in library information services, such as the House of Commons Library.[23]

There are great attractions in handling all forms of the vast quantities of information held by government departments through a computer-based system. An on-line information retrieval system which allows access by terminal to a computer store for both input and retrieval would allow the input of new records directly on to store for both easy correction of errors and immediate availability of information for a variety of users. Such systems are increasingly used by large organisations the world over and are available as a source of encouragement and warning. Something of the sort is probably necessary if the operational requirements of departments are to be reconciled with the demands of outside users under FOI without an excessive use of manpower and disruption of ordinary administrative routines. There will almost certainly be a gain to the department itself from a more flexible, versatile and accessible organisation of its own information and from the thorough and self-conscious review of information requirements which setting up the new system will entail. One benefit may be a reduction in what the Canadians call 'paperburden', the requirements on others to furnish information of which the department makes little or no use.

COSTS

It would be idle to pretend, however, that such a system could be introduced without major costs involving

(1) sophisticated programming systems;
(2) the creation of an index system;
(3) implementation of indexing even though this would not be done retrospectively;
(4) senior manpower required to establish criteria for access and

exemption in the first instance, and on a continuing basis to review marginal or doubtful cases;

(5) senior manpower to establish schedules for retention and disposal in collaboration with the PRO;

(6) provision of facilities for public access and the actual provision of information;

(7) resolution of conflicts between departments and citizens over access.

The major part of these costs will arise from setting up the new integrated system. These capital costs will undoubtedly be substantial, but it can be confidently anticipated that the new system will be both more economical and more efficient than the existing one. Government departments which handle large volumes of statistical or routine data have of course already adopted automatic data-processing techniques. The advantages of the application of new technology to administrative and policy work of a less structured kind are less well understood.

There are vast improvements in speed, accessibility, cost and permanence of storage which can already be realised over existing manual systems with the use of such technology; it is inconceivable that over the next few years government departments will not avail themselves of these advantages. The initial costs may seem formidable both in terms of equipment and of the intellectual effort required to devise the appropriate systems; the long-run savings, especially in manpower costs, of routine paper-handling will more than outweigh them.[24] The additional costs of building in a system for public access are likely to be marginal, though not negligible. They are in any event difficult if not impossible to quantify. Facilities for access and resolution of disputed claims for access depend, for instance, on the volume of demand for access and the number of disputes arising with departments which cannot be forecast. The most frightening estimates of cost have come from the United States, where loosely-drafted legislation, especially in relation to commercial confidentiality, has encouraged extensive litigation and where FOI was imposed on the existing administrative system without any prior attempt to reorganise records and with retrospective effect.[25] There is no need to repeat these mistakes.

Cost is not the critical factor. Sooner rather than later the advantages of new technology will make change inevitable; it might as well be a comprehensive and coherent reform. The present system of record-keeping is not notably efficient or cheap and is liable either to choke on its own product or survive by haphazard destruction. New systems of data-processing, storage and retrieval, already in partial use, could be extended with great advantage to the whole of government administration, policymaking and records management. The preservation of records for future use and arrangements for immediate public access could both be built into this system with minimal technical difficulty and at marginal extra cost, when considered against the scale of government's direct and indirect investment in information technology. The problems are not technical or financial, but political.

POSTSCRIPT

In the White Paper (Reform of Section 2 of the Official Secrets Act 1911, Cm 408), duly published in June 1988, Mr Hurd sprang one welcome surprise. He abandoned the conclusive ministerial certificate on the harm done by unauthorised disclosure in favour of judgement by a jury. But he limited the effect of this concession by reducing the test of harm and by making disclosure of four categories of information subject to no test of harm at all. In making the tests of harm specific to particular categories of information, Mr Hurd has moved from the Franks recommendation of 'serious injury', equivalent to a classification of 'Top Secret' or 'Secret', to terms such as 'likely to damage', 'prejudice', or 'jeopardise', which are equivalent to a classification of 'Confidential'. This brings vastly more information within the scope of the offences than was recommended by Franks or proposed in the Government's 1979 Bill. The offences for which there is no test of harm also bring a great range of information within the scope of criminal sanctions, much of it trivial. This will prolong uncertainty as to what can and cannot be disclosed without risk of prosecution and provide a continuing opportunity for selective prosecution by the Government of the kind we have witnessed recently in the treatment of various books on the security services. Finally, Mr Hurd has set his face against a defence of prior disclosure or any form of public interest defence, and has failed to grapple with the murky problem of what is meant by authorisation. Public rights of access to official information are dismissed in a sentence and the duty of civil servants to protect all information is emphasised and may be reinforced by changes to disciplinary codes and the civil law of confidence. In short Mr Hurd should not be mistaken for a liberal or even a moderate. He is the Head Prefect writ large.

Notes

1. Franks (1979), Lord Franks OM 'Disclosure and the Law'. Text of an Address given to a seminar on Open Government held at the Civil Service College on 13–15 November 1978. January 1979. CSC Working Paper, No. 5.
2. Justice, 'Freedom of Information', 1978.
3. Franks (1972), Report and Evidence of the Committee on Section 2 of the Official Secrets Act 1911. Cmnd 5104 (1972), Chairman Lord Franks.
4. The relevant White Papers are
Information and the Public Interest, Cmnd 4089 (1969).
Reform of Section 2 of the Official Secrets Act 1911, Cmnd 7285 (1978).
Open Government, Cmnd 7280 (1979).
5. Hansard, Volume 125, no. 73, Friday 15 January 1988, cl. 581–87.
6. Hansard, ibid., cl. 565.
7. This argument was rehearsed in an earlier debate on the committee stage of Mr Clement Freud's *Official Information Bill* in March 1979.
8. Hansard, ibid., cl. 625.
9. Hansard, ibid., cl. 566–67, *Initial Services Ltd v. Putterill (1968) 1QB, 396, 405*.
10. See, for instance, the interesting report produced by the Civil Service Department following the Sachsenhausen Case: *Legal Entitlements and Administrative Practices: A report by officials*, HMSO, London, 1962.
11. Armstrong, Sir Robert, *The Duties and Responsibilities of Civil Servants in relation to Ministers. Note by the Head of the Home Civil Service*, Cabinet Office, 25 February 1985, para. 11.
12. Recommendation No. R(81)19 1979.
13. Earlier versions of the Bill were introduced by Robin Cook MP, Michael Meacher MP and Sir Clement Freud as the *Official Information Bill* in the Parliament of 1974–79 and by Frank Hooley in 1980–81.
14. For a similar but much better-informed judgement see Patrick Nairne 'Policy-making in Public' in Richard A. Chapman and Michael Hunt (eds), *Open Government*, Croom Helm, London, 1987.
15. This matter is hotly disputed. Industrial corporations make a large number of requests about their competitors, but with what success is uncertain. They also spend thousands of dollars on specialist news sheets, which when examined contain nothing that could not have been found by a careful reading of the main financial press.
16. Bennett (1980): Colin Bennett and Peter Hennessy, *A Consumer's Guide to Open Government: Techniques for Penetrating Whitehall*, Outer Circle Policy Unit, March 1980.

17. For a fuller treatment see an earlier paper written with Lindy Whitehead, formerly Librarian of the RIPA, to whom I am indebted for initiation into the mysteries of information science, and published by the Areopagitica Educational Trust in *Public Access to Official Records – The Practical Issues*.
18. The Public Records system and its relations to FOI are concisely discussed in Michael Roper's 'Access to Public Records' in Richard A. Chapman and Michael Hunt (eds), *Open Government*, Croom Helm, London, 1987.
19. See for example:
    The Wilson Report (1981) *Modern Public Records: Selection and Access*, Report of a Committee, Chairman: Sir Duncan Wilson, Cmnd 8204, March 1981, and
    Bennett (1980), op. cit.
20. The Wilson Report, para. 72.
21. Knoppers (1980–81): 'Records Management in Canada: Freedom of Information and Privacy', Parts I and II: by Dr Jake V. Th. Knoppers, *Records Management Quarterly*, October 1980 and April 1981.
22. Treasury Committee (1979–80), Appendix 4: Promoting efficiency and the use of computers in government departments, *Civil Service Manpower Reductions*, Vol. II, Minutes of Evidence and Appendices HC 712–II.
23. Korner (1982): *Health Services Information Steering Group: NHS and DHSS First Report to the Secretary of State* (The Korner Report), HMSO, London, 1982.
    Fairey (1983): 'The Korner Report and its implementation', M. J. Fairey, *Hospital & Health Services Review*, July 1983.
    Menhennet (1982): '"Polis" in Parliament: computer-based information retrieval in the House of Commons Library', David Menhennet and Jane Wainwright, *Journal of Documentation*, 38(2), June 1982.
24. Examples of benefits attributable to existing computer and telecommunications systems against the manual systems they replaced are outlined in Annexe A of *Civil Service Manpower Reductions*: Treasury Committee (1979/80).
25. CSD (1979): *Disclosure of Official Information: A Report on Overseas Practice*, Civil Service Department, HMSO, London, 1979.

10 Making Government Responsible to Parliament

John Grigg

Hardly a minute passes without somebody, somewhere, referring to Westminster as the mother of Parliaments. But John Bright coined the phrase to describe England, not Westminster, and it is necessary to make the correction, because it has a more than pedantic significance. The country came first – and should always come first. Our Parliament did not create itself, and in the modern democratic age the membership of at least one House is determined by the people, to whom Parliament as a whole is ultimately responsible. Though it is right that our parliamentarians should exercise their own judgements and should not, when elected, behave as delegates, Parliament nevertheless has to satisfy the people that it is as well constituted, and working as well, as possible. It will not do for MPs and peers to be collectively satisfied with themselves.

The British political system depends upon common sense, goodwill and, above all, the vigilance of citizens. Unlike the US Constitution, it is not a theoretical construct, but an organism which has evolved over centuries from medieval kingship to a sort of democracy. Yet its essentially monarchical character remains, not only in the person of a now constitutional sovereign, but also in the powers of the Crown as wielded by a supposedly responsible executive. There is no formal separation of powers, as in the United States. The executive is part of the legislature and is, therefore, formally free to become an elected dictatorship, which is, indeed, how it sometimes appears. Parliament is meant to control the government of the day by vetting its actions, amending its legislation, and checking any tendency to abuse its power. But Parliament's capacity to do this effectively is not guaranteed by the nature of the system. On the contrary, it is subject to many practical limitations, which today are becoming more marked.

British governments are now more powerful, internally, than at any time since 1688; certainly more so than at the beginning of this century. Britain was then the most powerful country in the world, and British governments naturally carried more weight abroad than they do now. But since the First World War the purview and patronage of government within the country have been vastly extended, while Britain's world standing, at any rate since the Second World War, has greatly declined. Consequently, whereas Lord Salisbury had far more clout with foreigners than Mrs Thatcher has, she has far more clout with her own compatriots.

Has Parliament's power grown in proportion to that of the government since the early years of the century? Most honest observers would have to say that it has not. Indeed, it is hard to deny that Parliament has become, on the whole, more subservient. One reason is that the parliamentary timetable is not remotely adequate for dealing with the modern executive. Ministers have always had the big advantage that they, or at any rate their departments, have been on the job throughout the year, while Parliament has sat for only part of the year. But this advantage has, of course, been compounded by an enormous growth of state activity without any corresponding increase in the amount of time Parliament has been in session. In 1906 Parliament sat for about 160 days, and eighty-odd years later it still sits for about the same number of days annually (172 in 1985–6). How can a Parliament sitting for less than half the year hope to control a full-time modern government?

For months on end the Palace of Westminster is like an uninhabited stately home, with groups of tourists filing through its empty chambers, while MPs concentrate on their work as local welfare officers, attend to other business, or merely relax. But ministers nowadays hardly ever relax. They have become workaholics, without necessarily achieving better results than their more leisurely Edwardian predecessors.

True, MPs now put in longer hours while they are at Westminster. Earlier in the century their average daily stint was normally below 8 hours, but since 1964 it has become, in most sessions, 9 hours or more. From Mondays to Thursdays the House of Commons meets at 2.30 p.m. and sits until 10.30 p.m. or later: often much later. On Fridays it meets at 9.30 a.m. and adjourns at 3.0 p.m. The longer daily average in recent years is due, quite simply, to more late sittings on weekdays other than Fridays.

This is surely no improvement. Late sittings are, in principle, undesirable: bad for health, temper, judgement and family life. Debates and divisions after the hour when civilised men and women go home are an abomination. Midnight argument conducted by people who have been busy during the day is unlikely to be fruitful. Yet MPs cannot, like factory workers on night shift, afford to be out of circulation during the daylight hours. The odious practice of sitting late has been extended as an alternative to sitting for more days in the year. But surely a more sensible pattern of attendance would involve a larger number of days, and fewer unsocial hours.

Changing the timetable would undoubtedly help, but would by no means suffice, to bring the executive under proper parliamentary control. An even more serious matter than the relative absenteeism of Parliament has been the sapping of MPs' independence through the growth in the number of placemen in the House of Commons. This has been happening by gradual degrees, and so has escaped the attention it deserves. Yet it has brought about a state of affairs which, in 1900, would have seemed alarming and outrageous.

At that date, when Britain was a superpower ruling a quarter of the world, Lord Salisbury's government had a total strength of 64 ministers, including 17 Court appointments, many of which would soon cease to be political. In 1922, the Bonar Law government, with fewer courtiers but, on the other hand, ministers running new departments recently created by Lloyd George, such as Air, Labour, Transport and Health, had only 60 members. Two years later the first MacDonald government was, with 57 members, the smallest of modern times. In general, until the Second World War, the size of governments was kept within reasonable bounds.

But Churchill's wartime coalition began the process of ministerial inflation, and Attlee's 1945 government was over 80 strong. By 1970 Lord Wilson had increased the number to 98, and Lord Callaghan can claim the dubious distinction of having raised it above the century mark. There Mrs Thatcher has kept it, despite her vaunted opposition to overmanning and 'big government'.

Until the last war the ministerial complement was the same in almost every department of state: one senior and one junior minister. But in 1943 Churchill set what has turned out to be a disastrous precedent, in appointing a minister of state at the Foreign Office. In the circumstances of the time the appointment was justified, because the Secretary of State, Anthony Eden, being also a member of the War Cabinet and Leader of the House of Commons, was desperately overworked. But since then ministers of state, occupying the level between senior and junior ministers, and so neither one thing nor the other, have proliferated, until today there is at least one in every department, and often more than one.

It may not be unduly cynical to suggest that this intermediate tier of ministers is useful to prime ministers as a means of bringing more politicians on to the payroll, and of giving some of them higher status and pay without making them top ministers. Since at the same time not fewer, but more, under-secretaries have been created, it is hardly surprising that the total inflation of numbers has been so great. Some defend this ministerial hypertrophy on the grounds that more ministers are needed today to deal with the increased volume of departmental business; for instance, that a team of eight ministers is justified at the Department of the Environment, when that ministry has three major bills to promote. But we should remember that between 1906 and 1909 the Home Office sponsored seven major bills (Workmen's Compensation, Coal Mines Regulation, Trade Boards, Children, Probation of Offenders, Criminal Appeal and Prevention of Crime), with only two politicians, Herbert Gladstone and his under-secretary, Herbert Samuel, leading the department.

There is no evidence that the Parkinson's Law now applied to ministerial appointments has made for greater efficiency. Besides, who can seriously imagine that the prime motive for its application has been to improve the quality of government? A more obvious and compelling motive must, surely, have been to increase government's hold over the House of Commons. Beyond question that has been its effect. The enlargement of the ministerial payroll has tended to corrupt and weaken the House of Commons, all the more so as ministers are now overwhelmingly recruited from there. (Whereas Lord Salisbury's last Cabinet contained nine peers, there are only three in Mrs Thatcher's as I write.) Moreover, quite apart from all the MPs who are silenced by being given salaried jobs, there is also the outer penumbra of those who serve ministers as PPSs, or who merely hope for office at the next reshuffle. And, as if that were not bad enough, Mrs Thatcher has revived the habit – largely spurned, to his credit and cost, by Mr Heath – of bestowing knighthoods, etc. upon MPs who might otherwise be disaffected. Not, perhaps, since the eighteenth century has government maintained itself so shamelessly by the exercise of patronage within Parliament, or have placemen been so obtrusive in our political system.

Because there are now so many jobs going in the House of Commons, people tend to stand for it primarily, or even solely, with a view to obtaining office. This is a pity. At the beginning of the century, when the House of Commons had rather more members than it has today (because the whole of Ireland was still represented), and when the number of ministers drawn from it was much smaller, it was quite normal for a person to stand for Parliament with no serious hope, and certainly no expectation, of ever becoming a minister. The job of an MP was then seen as worthwhile for its own sake. It was, of course, a less demanding job than it is now, more especially at the constituency level. Though Parliament is still a part-time institution so far as its sessions are concerned, most MPs are now full-time professionals, if only as local ombudsmen. Yet to most of them the goal of their professional ambition is appointment to a government post, and unless the call comes they feel cheated, despised and frustrated.

In itself, it is no bad thing that politics should be treated as a profession rather than as a sport for gentlemen. In the past there may have been too many MPs whose approach to their work was amateurish. But it is against the interests of Parliament, and of the country, that the professionalism and honourable ambition of MPs should be as concentrated as it now is upon holding ministerial office. This concentration has the effect of destroying the informal balance of power within Parliament, which is a necessary alternative to the formal separation of powers that our system fails to provide.

How is the informal balance to be restored? No enthusiasm for restoring it is ever likely to be shown by the government of the day and its large Parliamentary retinue. Nor is anything to be expected from the official Opposition, the other party to what has become a traditional duopoly, which hopes in due course to enjoy again all the advantages of the system. Only if and when a new political force, committed to reforming the system, succeeds in winning power, will a thorough programme of Parliamentary regeneration be carried through. In the Commons this would, surely, need to include a resolution by the House limiting to, say, 60 or 65 the number of its members who, at any one time, could be holding ministerial office. It would be good, also, if the Commons were to resolve that honours awarded on the prime minister's advice should not be accepted by serving MPs. But no such programme of self-denial is likely for the time being.

Meanwhile the best hope of achieving some correction of the balance in favour of Parliament lies with the select committees which, eight years ago, were established (on lines proposed by the Commons' own committee on procedure) to correspond with, and to supervise, all the main departments of state. The setting-up of these new department-related committees owed much to active sponsorship by the then Leader of the House, Norman St John Stevas (now Lord St John of Fawsley), who expressed the hope that they would 'provide opportunity for closer examination of departmental policy', and that they would represent 'an important contribution to greater openness in government'. So far their achievements, though by no means negligible, have failed quite to live up to the bright promise of his words as he launched them; and it was perhaps symbolic that, not long afterwards, Mrs Thatcher dropped him from the Cabinet.

The main purpose of the committees is to give MPs the means to probe and interrogate government, including civil servants, with a rigour impossible in the traditional pantomime of Question Time. To some degree this purpose has been served, though the impact of the committees' inquisitorial work, so far, should not be exaggerated. Most of their reports are shelved without even a parliamentary debate. The government still has many ways to circumscribe and circumvent their efforts. For one thing, since MPs cannot be subpoenaed to testify – but only invited – it can never be obligatory for a minister to appear and justify his or her actions. Mrs Thatcher, for instance, could never have been forced to appear before the defence committee during the Westland hearings, even if a committee with a built-in Conservative majority had been willing to demand her attendance.

The theoretical case for giving MPs immunity from subpoena by select committee is, perhaps, open to question. Parliamentary privilege is very necessary to protect MPs against any external restraint upon their freedom to serve the public according to their lights. But should the privilege of individual MPs be allowed to override the authority of Parliament itself? Should even the prime minister, under our system, be free to avoid accounting to a Commons select committee for what he or she has done, or not done? In the United States the President cannot, indeed, be subpoenaed by a Congressional committee, but then he is a separate, and separately elected, power under the Constitution, embodying in himself the executive power of the Republic. There is no such justification for exempting the chief executive in our country. On the contrary, the theory of our constitution is that the whole government is not only part of Parliament, but collectively responsible to it. (The growing distance between theory and practice is the theme of this chapter.)

Ideally, select committees might be composed of the most suitable and qualified MPs, regardless of party. Yet the view that their composition should reflect party strengths in the House is defensible, quite apart from the argument of realism. All the same, to accept the present basis of membership is not to agree that it is right for the individuals representing the parties to be chosen, as they now are, by their party whips, subject only to endorsement by the whole House. It would be better, surely, if the House were to claim the initiative in the choice of members for the committees, within the party quotas, and better still if the choice could be by secret ballot, though that would be against the long-established principle of openness in Parliamentary votes. At the very least the committee members should be elected, in their due party proportions, by an open vote of all MPs. This would set a premium on candidates with independent minds and a readiness to act independently on behalf of Parliament and the national interest, rather than on candidates known to the whips as safe and dependable.

Even now, some MPs of spirit are to be found on select committees, either because the whips misjudged them or because the whips themselves were prepared to stretch a point. Occasionally, too, a list is amended under pressure from the whole House. This occurred in the case of Frank Field, Labour MP for Birkenhead, with the result that he became not just a member, but chairman, of the select committee on social services.

The case is noteworthy as illustrating both what is basically wrong in the present system and how it can, nevertheless, at times produce the right result. Mr Field knows as much about social services as anybody in the House of Commons; yet at the beginning of this Parliament he was not on the original list of Labour nominees for the social services committee, put forward by the Labour whips. It is easy to guess why. Though far from being a fellow-traveller of the right, he has opposed the left wing of his party with more courage and consistency than any of his party leaders. He is also that very rare phenomenon in contemporary politics, an MP who is content with the role of a backbencher and therefore indifferent to the lure of office, whether actual or prospective.

Chairmanship of the social services committee being allotted to Labour, it was rumoured that the party managers intended Audrey Wise to be chairman. This provoked a Conservative MP, Nicholas Winterton, into putting a motion on the Order Paper to the effect that Mrs Wise should be removed from the list of members, and Mr Field substituted. The Labour whips then asked Mr Field if he would like to serve on the committee and, when he said he would, a Labour nominee (not Mrs Wise) was switched to another committee and a place thus found for him. The committee in turn elected him chairman, though the Labour left made a strenuous attempt at a party meeting to block his chairmanship. If the committee's composition had been decided by a vote of the whole House, as I have suggested it should be, he would most probably have become a member in the first place, without any delay.

Another form of select committee is the select standing committee which may be authorised to take the committee stage of a bill, with the power to call expert witnesses. But this can only happen by permission of the House, which in practice means the Government, so long as Parliament is ruled by a disciplined single-party majority. To date the recently devised procedure of referring the committee stage of a complex bill to a select standing committee has been used on only five occasions, so it cannot be said that the experiment has been carried very far. Under different conditions it might be carried much further, and with beneficial results.

The work of select committees is already very demanding in time and effort, and may well become considerably more so as their potential develops. If their members were elected by the House rather than, in effect, appointed by the whips, it would seem fair that they should receive an addition to their Parliamentary salaries; and the case for paying the chairmen of such committees, who have a heavy workload if they are doing the job properly, is anyway strong. An alternative career structure to that controlled and exploited by the party leaders would thus be available to MPs. As committee members they would be paid as officers of the House, and their freedom to serve the House would be correspondingly enhanced.

If and when proceedings in the Commons are televised, as they now at last may be within measurable time, it will be most important that the cameras should record what goes on in committees as well as what happens on the floor of the House. The detailed work of the Commons, as of any other public body, can of course be very boring; but it is not always so, and in any case information and argument of far more substance is likely to emerge from select committee hearings or the committee stage of bills than from routine knockabout turns such as Prime Minister's Questions. Television should help the elected chamber to recapture the central place that it ought to have in the nation's consciousness, and so help to correct the present disequilibrium between MPs and ministers. For while the Commons were, for more than twenty years, fighting shy of television, ministers were making ample use of it to sell their policies and project their personalities. (Some backbenchers are, of course, regular TV performers, but they are not necessarily the most important ones, and anyway they appear much less often than senior ministers.)

Television has done a lot for the House of Lords. Indeed, so long as the Lords were the only parliamentarians being televised, their reputation inevitably grew at the Commons' expense, and the myth that they have better debates than the Commons gained ground. That myth will hardly survive comparison of the two Chambers by the viewing public. All the same, the House of Lords has distinctive merits as well as serious defects. Parliament needs a Second Chamber, to revise legislation emerging, often in a semi-digested form, from the House of Commons; to air matters for which the Commons may not have enough time, or to which they are not able to bring the same range of expertise; and to provide representation for groups and interests that are not adequately represented through the electoral process.

The element of nomination in the way our Second Chamber is composed is a major strength, because it enables people who have not made politics their career, but who have a clear capacity to serve the state, to be recruited for government while becoming members of one House of Parliament, as ministers have to be. If, as some would wish, we had had an all-elected Second Chamber, it is unlikely that the country would have had the services of Lord Woolton as Minister of Food during the last war; and many other examples could be cited of valuable ministers who would have felt themselves debarred by elective politics. Another good argument for nomination is that it potentially allows groups that suffer from our electoral system, more especially in its present unreformed state, to be given proper representation in at least one House of Parliament. Ethnic minorities and, above all, women are obvious cases in point, though one has to say that proper representation for them is as yet no more than potential, grossly insufficient use having so far been made of the opportunity to send representatives of them to the House of Lords.

Another reason for dismissing the idea of an all-elected Second Chamber, and surely the clinching one, is that the House of Commons would never agree to establish such a rival to itself. For that reason alone it is pointless to spend any more time discussing the matter. But, granted the need for a House that is largely, if not wholly, composed on principles other than the elective, is the present composition of the House of Lords right? Most certainly it is not. The fact that it is illogical is neither here nor there, because the English are rightly suspicious of logic. But certain features of the present composition of our Second Chamber are as harmful in practice as they are indefensible in theory.

One, which many have long recognised as a flaw, is the unrestricted right of hereditary peers to sit in the Upper House, and to enjoy all the privileges and perquisites (the latter by no means negligible) of attendance. Until the 1963 Peerage Act only male peers of the United Kingdom (by far the largest segment of the total) were automatically entitled to sit; but under that measure, which attracted most notice for the provision enabling peers to disclaim for life, the right to sit was extended to the whole Scottish peerage and to hereditary peeresses. Previously those categories, like the Irish peerage, were denied hereditary seats in Parliament, though free to vote in Parliamentary elections and to stand for the House of Commons; and the Scottish peerage had, in addition, the right to elect sixteen of its number to sit as representative peers in the House of Lords. Since 1963 all hereditary peers and peeresses, except the Irish, have been entitled to sit. The net effect of the 1963 Act was, therefore, substantially to reinforce the hereditary basis of the Second Chamber.

Defenders of the hereditary principle, as applied to the Upper House, use four arguments: that hereditary peers are more independent than those who are nominated, or who might be elected; that, because some peers inherit early in life, their right to sit gives the House a welcome injection of youth, which would otherwise be absent; that the hereditary peerage is, in a sense, more representative than any other element in Parliament, because it is a random group of citizens, rather like a jury; and, finally, that if breeding counts for so much in the world of horseracing, it must have an equal relevance to the world of politics.

Taking the arguments in turn, one can say of the first that it is demonstrably false. Hereditary peers do not, in fact, show more political independence than other peers. Independence is a quality of mind and character that a privileged background does not necessarily confer. Anyone who looks at history with an unclouded eye can see that some of the most servile of party hacks have always been found among the hereditary peers. The argument about youth has some validity, though I shall soon be suggesting a better way to achieve the same result. Hereditary peers representative, like a jury? There are complaints that even juries are not a true cross-section, tending to be too middle-class. But at their very worst they are more broadly based, socially, than the hereditary peerage, which can best be described as a group randomly representing the upper and upper-middle classes. As for the argument that political talent is hereditary like that of racehorses, there is of course some truth in it; clearly there are political families, as there are, for instance, musical, medical and cricketing families. But in almost every sphere other than the House of Lords hereditary talent has to prove itself in action. A racehorse, however good its breeding, has to race; its name is not automatically put up in the frame. And who, as Nancy Astor pertinently asked, would think of having an hereditary cricket team? There may be a case for having a limited number of hereditary peers elected by their peers to sit, as the representative Scottish peers used to be. But unrestricted entitlement is, surely, a nonsense.

If automatic hereditary membership of the House is objectionable, the proliferation of life peerages is no less so. The principle of peerages for life was established in 1876, but until 1958 was confined to the Law Lords. In the latter year it was extended to men and women without restriction. Obviously the 1958 Act has had some good effects, though its use by successive prime ministers has so far been unimaginative, as I have already indicated. But above all it was a mistake to flood the House with more life members. Already, while it was virtually all-hereditary, it had a markedly geriatric character, because hereditary peers sit for life. But with the addition of a large and ever-growing body of specifically life peers, appointed for the most part in the late afternoon or early evening of their lives, the House has taken on an air of oppressive senility.

This is not to say that there should be a statutory age limit for peers. There are individual cases of very old people who, like the late Lord Stockton, are thoroughly worthy of seats in Parliament. But on the whole the contribution that people can make diminishes as time passes, and the value of a public body is unlikely to be enhanced by the presence in it of too many dotards. Among public bodies the House of Lords is, to put it mildly, unusual in consisting overwhelmingly of members who have tenure for life. Tenure for a longish time is, indeed, for obvious reasons desirable, and there should be no limit to the age at which a person might be appointed to the Second Chamber. But appointment for a set period – say, ten years – would enable people of all ages, young, middle-aged and old, to be appointed without the dangers and disadvantages inseparable from permanent tenure. The appointment of younger people would, in particular, be facilitated by this change, because at present there is a natural reluctance to appoint them for what may be half a century or more.

An interesting category of peer that deserves to be much enlarged is the *ex officio* category. At present this consists only of the 26 senior bishops of the Church of England, who sit in the House of Lords so long as they hold their sees, but retire when they vacate them. Would it not be a good idea to admit others on the same principle: for example, the governor of the Bank of England, the general secretary of the TUC, the president of the Royal Society, and the chairman of the National Trust? Among religious leaders of denominations other than Anglican, the Chief Rabbi has recently been given a life peerage. But might it not be more appropriate for the holder of his office to sit in the House of Lords by virtue of being Chief Rabbi, and for the same right to belong to the Roman Catholic Archbishop of Westminster? The beauty of *ex officio* membership is that it brings people into Parliament for as long as they are occupying important posts outside it, but for no longer. Too many peers now become active in the House of Lords only when they cease to be active outside. (One who presided over a great national institution once told me he could not attend much at the time, because he was too busy, but that he looked forward to attending more when he retired – a good illustration of what is wrong with the present set-up.)

One further crucial issue relating to the Second Chamber remains to be considered. Should members of the House of Lords necessarily be lords in the titular sense? As things are now, there is a most unfortunate confusion between those who are ennobled for outstanding public service and those who go to the Upper House either to make up party strengths there or as a form of gratuity after long but far from brilliant careers in the House of Commons. It is really quite absurd that a former prime minister like Lord Callaghan of Cardiff should receive exactly the same form of peerage as a former chief whip; and that Lord Jenkins of Hillhead, who has been Home Secretary, Chancellor of the Exchequer, president of the European Commission and co-founder of a new party, should not be differentiated in titular degree from Lord Jenkins of Putney, a former minister for the arts (and a pretty moderate one at that).

It seems not only right, but imperative, that when a peerage is awarded as a particularly high honour it should be seen, unmistakably, as such. And it is hard to think of any better way to make sure of this than to stop the award of titular peerages for any other reason. In other words, membership of the Second Chamber should not, in itself, carry a lordly title, but should be indicated by the letters LP (Lord or Lady of Parliament) after the member's name. And if it should be thought that members of an institution called the House of Lords must, on that account, be called Lord This or Lady That, let it be noted that a commoner can hold the office of Lord President of the Council or Lord Privy Seal; in fact, nowadays usually does. So why should Lords and Ladies of Parliament not be commoners as well?

Whether or not peerages awarded to honour people of exceptional merit should be transmitted to heirs is a separate question, not to be discussed here. Equally peripheral is the question whether or not they should be graded, as peerages traditionally have been. Mrs Thatcher has recommended the conferring of one hereditary earldom and two hereditary viscountcies (the two latter, however, lacking apparent heirs), so she may be moving, though in a very gingerly fashion, back towards the traditional system. But whatever happens about peerages in the titular sense, it is essential that they should not be conferred upon anybody and everybody who is sent to the House of Lords, and that those who inherit them should not automatically inherit seats there. Peers and peeresses of first creation might, however, be entitled to sit for life.

This chapter has been concerned with what is wrong with Parliament rather than with all that is right: inevitably, because the theme of the whole book is reform and renewal. But the chapter has been written with a strong, if somewhat concealed, sense of reverence for an institution that is unique and precious, though at present too little studied by the public at large. Parliamentary reports, even in quality newspapers, have become very scrappy, and circulation of the official reports, outside Parliament itself, is almost non-existent. The total daily print of the House of Commons Hansard is between 4000 and 5000; of the House of Lords Hansard between 2900 and 3000 (both figures varying according to the business). The Lords' weekly Hansard has a print of 700, while the Commons' fortnightly edition prints 1240. These are pathetic figures. With television making people more aware of Parliament as a whole, it should be possible to increase them substantially, though only if a determined effort is made to find sales outlets additional to HM Stationery Office.

The main argument of this chapter has been that Parliament needs to regain a lot of the power that it has lost to the executive, and for this purpose electoral reform, which is the subject of another chapter, is no less vital than the internal reform of Parliament. Some will argue that any further curbing of the executive would be perverse, because the advantages of strong government, always hard to establish in a democracy, would in the process be sacrificed. I can only reply that the changes I have proposed would leave the government, and more especially the head of the government, with as much power and patronage as are consistent with the survival of a true Parliamentary democracy.

V Improving Government

11 Whitehall and the Civil Service

William Plowden

Because this article is one in a collection dealing with constitutional questions, it is selective in its coverage of Whitehall and the civil service. It has little to say about the Financial Management Initiative, or – except by implication – about the recruitment, training or career management of civil servants, though there is certainly a lot that can be said on these subjects. Nor does it touch on the recruitment, training or career management of ministers, about which there is probably even more to be said. It says little about the hundreds of thousands of civil servants in junior, executive and technical grades. It concentrates, as far as it is meaningful to do so, on the character of the *senior* civil service: on the relationship between this character and the role of this group as an instrument of constitutional government, on the ways in which that character seems to be changing, on some of the reasons for those changes, and on the implications of those changes for the nature of government and, perhaps, for the framework of conventions and constraints on government that may be needed in a just society. These matters are important in all states. In Britain, where the power of the executive has increased, is increasing, and shows no signs of being diminished, the character and behaviour of the civil service is of quite fundamental importance.

One familiar model of a civil service sees it as helping to achieve the purposes of democratic government in two closely related ways. First, it acts as an effective instrument for democratically-elected politicians to carry out their policies. Unlike ministers, most of whom are professional politicians but basically amateurs in government, civil servants are professionals in government. They are intellectually rigorous, ingenious, lifetime-careerists, highly-motivated, working as advisers and executives in a close partnership with ministers, whose ultimate authority and responsibility is accepted and acceptable on the assumption that the partnership is a close one. The effectiveness of the civil service rests partly on its professionalism and on the existence of shared values that that implies. The nature of these values underlies the second distinctive contribution made by the civil service to democratic government. It helps to maintain such government precisely because its values are democratic values, derived from and informed by civil servants' lifetime involvement in government. It is the willing instrument of Ministers in all normal and foreseeable circumstances. At the margin, however, and operating within closely defined limits, it would if need be act as an informal check on unconstitutional or improper behaviour. Its *permanence* guarantees that it would never behave like some of the outsiders parachuted into Washington with an American president. Its *professional ethic* is an even stronger guarantee against the kind of perversion that has overtaken civil services under totalitarian regimes.

Exactly the same model of the civil service is sometimes viewed rather differently. From another perspective, the civil service is portrayed as a secluded elite, with its own particular and largely self-interested values and objectives. Its main contributions to the processes of government are, first, to manipulate ministers and, second, to obstruct them or to distort their instructions. Its relationship with elected ministers is less one of partnership than of rivalry. Sir John Hoskyns and Tony Benn are at one in believing that the civil service, in its present form, cannot and will not implement the policies of a radical government. From this analysis they derive an alternative model of a civil service tamed, subject to much closer and more direct political control, more fluid at senior levels and consequently more variable in its policy stances.

These are both well-established, almost 'traditional', views of the civil service. Both, in their different ways, still inform much thinking about the civil service and ways in which it might be changed. But thinking today is also influenced by two other now widely-held beliefs about what has happened to the civil service under the present government. The first belief is that Mrs Thatcher has 'politicised' the civil service. She is said to have purged senior levels of any officials likely to dissent with her policies or even to offer advice about the possible problems to which they may give rise. The result is that the service has become a totally uncritical, subservient and pliable instrument for any policy, good or bad, advocated by Ministers. In short, she is moving towards the second model.

The second belief, which overlaps and in part underpins the first, is that the present administration has, through its attitudes and its substantive policies, irretrievably damaged the public standing and the private self-esteem (sc. morale) of the civil service. The result is that it is on the way to becoming a much less effective instrument for this or any other government.

The first of these beliefs, and to a lesser extent the second, are today staple fare of dinner-table conversation in Hampstead or Clapham. Both, however, need to be tested against, not to say controlled for, the views of their holders about the basic policies and philosophy of the present administration. Is it inherently worse obediently to implement the instructions of a radical Conservative administration than those of its Labour or even Alliance equivalent? That is not, per se, unconstitutional behaviour. Viewed objectively, the truly unconstitutional bureaucracy is that which arrogates to itself decisions about the acceptability, or even the practicability, of policies, right or left: only a very fine line divides the elitist, obstructive bureaucrat (my second model) from the heroic guardian of liberal values outlined in my first. If the high morale and self-esteem of the civil service rested on its belief that it could frustrate the purposes of governments of which it disapproved, then the sooner its pride was punctured, the better.

If one thus drains the assertions about 'politicisation' of their unspoken ideological content, there is much less to them. When my Institute set up a working party to enquire into what was currently happening to top jobs in Whitehall, I thought that we might find evidence of some politicisation in the strict sense that Ministers were over-riding the merit system so as to appoint officials (or indeed outsiders) more sympathetic to government ideology. The group was offered virtually no evidence to this effect.

It concluded, very broadly, that ministers have in fact been interviewing to secure the appointment of a certain *type* of person. (It is an additional complication that such appointments now seem more often to be influenced by accidents of chance and of personal impressions, but it would be very hard to demonstrate that any of them were improper.)

The group concluded, secondly, that the preferred type is often, in shorthand, the 'can-do' type rather than the more traditional wily, often cautious, self-consciously 'political', counsellor. In at least some parts of Whitehall the civil servant as adviser is no longer required. What is wanted, instead, is the will and the capacity to *execute*. (The development of this capacity is a major aim of the Financial Management Initiative.[1])

All the evidence suggests that the Central Policy Review Staff was abolished primarily because it had become seen – incorrectly – as a leaky liability, but there cannot in any case have been much future for a central staff whose task was to review policy. (A Central Programme Implementation Unit might have had more of a chance.) Some Ministers in the present government have made it clear that *they* will provide all the advice that they need on policy. The task of their officials is, in classic Weberian style, to get on and put policy into practice. Even if one finds this an acceptable division of roles, it is bound to be somewhat disheartening for civil servants whose expectations and experience alike have led them to believe that they are nothing if not confidential advisers to ministers. (It has to be said that there are, by all accounts, several ministers of whom all this is not true.)

The view that the current condition of the civil service is wholly due to the present government also needs examination. There are undoubtedly problems with recruitment, resignations, demotivation and so on. But I suggest that these are neither peculiar to this country, nor solely due to the actions of the present government. They are at least in part functions of a worldwide rethink of the role of the state, and of a consequent retrenchment of public services. In Britain the process goes back at least to 1976, when the then Labour government first tried to cut back on public spending and public sector manpower. Even more broadly, they are also partly the result of changing values and attitudes among younger professionals. These changes include, in particular, a much less ready acceptance of the idea of the *lifetime* career. People joining the civil service in the 1980s, like people joining many other professions, are in no sense committed to it, as to a vocation; their attitude is that if in 3, or 5, or 10 years they feel they will be better off elsewhere, they will move. As long ago as 1981, in an article in *Public Administration*, a young civil servant wrote

> Compared to the prewar period, today's civil service is much younger, less stable and committed, and less motivated by an ethic of public service. Many, if not most, civil servants are not particularly attracted to their work or to the civil service as a career but see it just as a job . . . They neither meet nor identify with senior officials; nor do they share the same outlook or experience.[2]

He was writing mainly about the clerical and executive grades, but I believe that these attitudes are now found at many levels. They are certainly reflected in informal opinion surveys which I have for several years carried out among the Administration Trainees whom I teach at the Civil Service College.

However, there can be no doubt that many of Whitehall's problems today *are* due to the actions of the present government. It is responsible for the climate of contempt for public service and public servants so prevalent since 1980. This has not only been damaging in itself. It has also been a context which has exaggerated the significance of specific episodes – especially when taken together with the philosophy that civil servants are merely executive agents for ministers, not advisers – subordinates, not collaborators. This is certainly not the first administration to withhold information from Parliament, and the Ponting affair was as much a matter of personalities as of principles. But it was an affair which many people saw as symbolising a current malaise. It damaged, in various degrees, everybody involved in it, including the civil service as an institution. Sir Robert Armstrong's subsequent first memorandum of February 1985, with its heavy emphasis on the loyalty owed to Ministers by civil servants, and its failure even to hint at the possibility of reciprocal obligations by ministers, made matters immeasurably worse.[3] Again, this is certainly not the first administration to use civil servants as pawns in backstage political infighting. But few battles have moved centre-stage with such ludicrous speed as did the Westland affair. Once again, this was widely seen as exemplifying a relationship which was going badly wrong. Once again, it damaged the civil service as an institution as much as it damaged individuals.

The role of the Cabinet Secretary has been both part of the context and has been central to some specific episodes. The transfer to Sir Robert Armstrong of the post of Head of Civil Service was one aspect of a deliberate shift in the emphasis of civil service personnel management. This shift implicitly de-emphasised the notion of the civil service as a profession – with a professional ethic of its own. This latter point was expressed in the Armstrong memorandum – both in its original form and in the revised version issued in December 1987:

> The Civil Service has no constitutional personality or responsibility separate from the duly constituted government of the day.[4]

The implication was that the civil service was more of a loose federation of groups of managers – of services for employment, or the environment, or industry. This was underlined by Sir Robert

Armstrong's replies to the subcommittee of the Treasury and Civil Service Committee about the nature of his responsibilities as head of the civil service:

> Some of those who comment on [the combination of posts] perhaps have an exaggerated idea of the extent of the responsibilities of the head of the Civil Service. Departments are managed by their permanent secretaries, and the head of the civil service cannot second-guess the permanent secretaries on the management of their departments. His regular functions are really confined to advising the Prime Minister on appointments and honours. It takes up some of my time but I do not think it takes up a quarter of my time and it could be less than that for those functions.[5]

He probably had little option but to reply in this vein. But neither the reply, nor the situation it revealed, can have reassured civil servants concerned about their interests *as civil servants*. Suppressing the post of head of the civil service, and combining it with that of the Cabinet Secretary – the Prime Minister's 'Man Friday', in Lord Bancroft's words – meant that the civil service was bereft of visible leadership at a time when leadership was most needed – a time of fundamental change and of challenge to the established values of the profession. Suppressing the post also symbolised and exacerbated the longstanding low status and professional weakness of civil service *central* personnel management, just about able to cope during times of expansion and of consensus about professional values, but often out of its depth in a period of retrenchment and of challenge to consensus. Personnel managers and senior administrators – who are indeed largely the same people – have both been equally slow to take account of the perceptions of their juniors and of the gradual changes in the aspirations of the next generation of officials. One weakness of both versions of the Armstrong memorandum was their implicit assumption of a continuing vocational ideal of the civil service. I believe that this simply does not make sense to many of those to whom it was addressed.

For the same general reasons I doubt if there is widespread confidence in the provisions for appeals by any civil servant whose professional obligations create for him a crisis of conscience. The Treasury and Civil Service Committee, in its inquiry into the duties and responsibilities of Ministers and civil servants, discussed at some length the case for establishing an appeals mechanism external to and independent of the official hierarchy. They finally decided against this, though with some misgivings, emphasising 'the important arguments for a system of external review.'[6] The government, not surprisingly, agreed with the Committee's recommendation though not with its misgivings.[7] The second Armstrong memorandum prescribes a wholly internal procedure, culminating in the Cabinet Secretary. (The memorandum added, indefensibly in my view, that if the matter could not thus be resolved, a civil servant still unwilling to obey instructions must resign and must still say nothing in public, ever.[8])

I have argued that the changes and strains apparent in Whitehall are due partly to the times, partly to the actions of the present government. I am not for a moment suggesting that those changes are all bad – or indeed that some of them go far enough. I am concerned simply with their constitutional implications, given conventional views about the constitutional role of the civil service.

I think I can detect among senior officials three salient groups, each responding rather differently to the pressures and challenges which I have described. All three types of response are, historically, unfamiliar. They correspond quite nicely to the threefold typology of consumer responses to firms posted by the economist Albert Hirschman in his book *Exit, Voice and Loyalty*.[9] Hirschman argued that classical microeconomics had identified two main responses to a seller by its customers. If satisfied with their purchases, they remained loyal to it. If dissatisfied, they made their exit to purchase from another vendor. Hirschman pointed out that there was a third group – dissatisfied customers who did not quietly exit but who raised their voices in complaint, demanding compensation and/or their money back.

In today's civil service there is one group which chooses EXIT. This includes both those who leave because they were never committed to a lifetime in the service and those who leave with regret, terminally demotivated by anxieties about pay, promotion, status and general change. The Efficiency Unit says that yet others leave because they are given little personal responsibility and see little prospect of acquiring more as they are promoted. The second group are a kind of EXIT/LOYALTY hybrid. Many of them are almost as dissatisfied as members of the EXIT group but, whether from a sense of vocational obligation, or because they lack transferable skills or the will to move, stay on – but operating in what might be called a 'damage-limitation' mode. That is to say, they do what is required of them but without enthusiasm and, related to this, without great expectations of preferment for the time being. Thus they are in one sense LOYAL. At the same time, they have made a kind of internal EXIT.

The third group are the truly LOYAL – those who, in contrast to both the other groups, are positively in tune with the present age – for reasons of temperament, policy stance, ideology or simply the accident of having been at some moment in the right place at the right time. Executive types, they welcome the new emphasis on action, as little sicklied o'er as possible with the pale cast of thought. The wind is in their sails, and they enjoy the sensation. They are enthusiasts. Both their preferment, and their style of administration, are among the things to which the internal EXITers object.

If this analysis is correct, it means that there can be no possible validity to the traditional model of the senior civil service mentioned at the beginning of my talk – a homogeneous profession, unified by shared values and commitment to a common vocational ideal: non-zealous, politically sensitive, cautious, ready and willing to serve virtually any legitimate government with dedication even if without enthusiasm, but intuitively aware of the limits to service and prepared – to cite Hirschman's third and last category – to VOICE disapproval of actions that go beyond those limits. There is not much sign of VOICE at all; it is fairly firmly discouraged, and kept wholly within the family, by the Armstrong memorandum.

I observe parenthetically that it is not at all clear what the ideal civil servant should look like. What should he be good at? Is he in fact any good at it? Can he be made to be good at it, especially if 'it' is management? Will he not always be inferior to his counterparts, *real* managers, in the private sector? Does public sector management require no special skills and insights? These doubts are the down-side of the shift to 'managerialism'. They seem to me likely to undermine the civil service's status, motivation, morale and competence. Ending them is a major task for civil service leadership. This is not the kind of task which has been well done in the civil service in the past. Obviously it cannot be done by civil servants in opposition to, or even in isolation from, ministers. Part of the task of civil service leaders now is to persuade ministers to take a more constructive responsibility for the service.

But that is something of an aside. This chapter is concerned more with the constitutional than with the managerial implications of this polarisation, fluidity, uncertainty in the civil service. Whatever the defects of the classical model of the civil service, it is implicitly built into the view taken by many satisfied observers of the British constitution. They argue, in effect, that despite the enormous power of the executive, the system is self-regulating. The civil service may, on the one hand, be conservative, cautious, elitist, amateurish, Sir Humphreyish, part of the British disease diagnosed by Martin Wiener[10] and Corelli Barnett[11] among many others – but, on the other, part of its strength is a unifying tradition, a professional ethic and an accepted code of behaviour – unwritten but real – which between them virtually guarantee constraints on governmental extremity. At the RIPA conference four years ago Michael Elliott argued that the civil service was the least bad available constraint on arbitrary or unconstitutional government.[12] He has recently suggested that the civil service, in this respect, is a 'busted flush'.[13] Others disagree: they claim that the civil service still has enormous capacity to obstruct ministerial initiatives. Even if this is true in some contexts, it is patently untrue in others. In any case, it does not address Michael Elliott's point: even if the civil service were still liable to frustrate policy changes of which it disapproved, would it necessarily resist actions which the rest of us might regard as arbitrary, unconstitutional or threatening to the rights of individuals?

I am not sure that it would. The constraints on the power of the executive under the British constitution are largely conventional – which tends to mean uncodified and unwritten. Such conventions range from the strong form of widely accepted precepts, challenge to which would be likely to precipitate a crisis – for example, that the Monarch should nominate as Prime Minister the person most likely to be able to command a majority in the House of Commons. At the other extreme, they can take the weaker form of merely customary behaviour – for example, that parties should foreshadow in their election manifestoes major policy changes which they propose to introduce if they win.

Conventions in this weaker sense also regulate the internal working of government, as of so many other British institutions. What Ministers may demand of their officials, how the latter should respond, what constitutes proper behaviour on the part of either, are all questions to which governments of all parties have been palpably reluctant to attempt definitive answers. The Prime Minister, introducing the first Armstrong memorandum, was at pains to say,

> This note does not and cannot discuss the corresponding responsibilities which Ministers have in relation to civil servants.[14]

However, the Treasury and Civil Service Committee managed to provoke a statement about these matters which was quoted in the second version.[15] The civil service Establishment Officers' Guide famously used to say (perhaps it still does) that it has never

> been thought necessary to lay down a precise code of conduct because civil servants jealously maintain their professional standards. In practice the distinctive character of the British civil service depends largely on the existence and maintenance of a general code of conduct which, although to some extent intangible and unwritten, is of very real importance.[16]

Despite the urging of the First Division Association, and to a lesser extent of the RIPA, there is still no code of ethics for civil servants. Still less is there anything equivalent to the basic legislation, found in other countries, defining the contractual rights and obligations of civil servants. Civil servants, I might add, are in general fairly unreflective on these matters. If pressed, they will tend either to deny the existence of problems in this sphere or to assert that, if problems did arise, any professional would know how to cope with them.

As Patrick McAuslan and others have argued, the application of these conventions, the style as well as the substance of British government, is greatly affected by the existence, in reserve, of the ill-defined powers of the Prerogative.[17] These allow the executive's will to prevail in circumstances where, in other systems of government, some effective constitutional check might have been applied. This exacerbates the delusion of British civil servants and ministers, understandable and dangerous, and shared with all others who wield governmental power, that one of the main tests of good government is that the will of the executive shall prevail. It exacerbates the tendency to interpret conventions of all kinds in ways likely to ensure that objective.

For these reasons, I have always had great doubts about the claim for the civil service as constitutional check. It reflects a complacency, indeed a naivety, about British institutions which history has all too often shown to be misplaced. In these changing times the claim looks increasingly unconvincing. I have suggested that the senior civil service may be polarising into separate groups. Two of them are, in different ways, making their EXIT from a system which no longer commands their confidence. Meanwhile the third, LOYAL, group exploits the relative freedom of action available to it. It is working within a system of rewards, and an administrative style, which emphasises enterprise, action, short-term results, economy and efficiency, at the relative expense of consultation, reflection, research, equity, accountability and consideration of side-effects. It has – presumably – accepted official guidance emphasising the civil servant's linked duties of loyalty to ministers and eternal silence.

Some may disagree with my analysis of what is happening in terms of the EXIT/NO VOICE/LOYALTY trichotomy. But as a statement of how things are at present *intended* to develop, I believe my characterisation of the LOYAL group to be pretty accurate. Like all other civil servants, the LOYAL group has no explicit code of behaviour which might provide criteria against which to test ministerial instructions and possible responses to these. Some observers, inside as well as outside Whitehall, believe that members of the group have already gone beyond acceptable implicit limits. However seductive the approval of senior ministers for officials willing to cut corners and get on with things, these critics argue, it is the professional duty of civil servants to point out to ministers any flaws, or unintended consequences of their policies. This may be uncomfortable; it may even endanger promotion; but it has to be done, because if civil servants do not do it in private nobody else can do it as effectively in public. The critics complain that some civil servants, hoping to fly high and higher, are failing in this duty.

If this is the situation, it is worrying in that it increases the chance that governments will do unthought-through things that they, and we, will later regret. It is clearly unsatisfactory for those civil servants who feel strongly that they have expert advice to offer on the making of policy, and who believe that their expertise is now being used only to put into effect policies largely determined elsewhere (e.g. in the Centre for Policy Studies or the Institute of Economic Affairs). These are valid points, which should be taken seriously. But I do not think that they add up to constitutional objections. It is the duty of governments to identify problems and define priorities and to choose the most appropriate administrative instruments and styles. They are fully entitled to full control of the civil service, and to change its values if they wish and are able. If the ability to manage is seen as important, then civil servants must be given managerial skills and structures within which to exercise them. My own priorities include making the senior civil service more aware of the untidy real world outside Whitehall, London and the South-East. I have also long wanted to see a civil service more responsive to changing ministers and to changing circumstances, with more movement in and out at all levels, more use by ministers of external advisers and more political influence over senior postings. I would add only that if one approves of this in principle one must allow it to constitutional governments of any party, including parties which one may not support. Beware of the conjugation, 'I am responsive; you are uncritical; he is politicised.'

But if developments of the kind now in train make governments more able to get things done, it is all the more important that there be adequate constraints to prevent the wrong things being done. I do sometimes wonder what are the effective limits to civil service obedience, loyalty and silence. How would serving officials, let alone the rest of us, know when those limits had been reached or overstepped and what would they do if they were? If internal constraints on arbitrary behaviour by governments are weak, and growing weaker, how adequate are the external constraints? The executive in Britain is one of the most powerful, and least accountable, in any advanced society in the world.

The whole thrust of the current efficiency strategy is to push the activities of civil service managers beyond day-to-day accountability to ministers and to Parliament. That is also the logic of the recent report by the Prime Minister's Efficiency Unit 'Improving Management in Government: the Next Steps'. That report includes a remarkably vague and unsatisfactory chapter about accountability; it argues that those future non-ministerial 'agencies' which – on the model of the Manpower Services Commission – are to remain parts of departments, will need 'a convention that the heads of executive agencies would have delegated authority from their Ministers for operations of the agencies within the framework of policy directives and resource allocations prescribed by Ministers'. Agencies outside departments would need 'appropriate forms of accountability to Ministers and to Parliament'.[18]

If forty years' experience of the Morrisonian public corporation is any guide, the outcome is likely to be continued confusion about the location of ultimate responsibility for specific actions, and difficulty in calling anyone to account for anything. It is, unfortunately, no compensation that these agencies will be answerable to Parliamentary Select Committees and to the Ombudsman – institutions which, whatever their merits as agents for scrutiny and comment, are unfortunately quite toothless when it comes to securing redress for government actions. If there is not to be effective current political control over these and existing structures, are there adequate arrangements for what might loosely be called audit (in a full and effective sense), review and the redress of grievance? The absence of the first ought to imply the stronger presence of the other three – not, as so often, for example, in the case of the police, the absence of all.

I do not think the arrangements are adequate. I can suggest palliatives, but if there are to be radical changes in the style and structure of the executive there must be some radical thinking about the framework within which the executive operates. I hope that the other articles in this collection will contribute to that thinking.

Notes

1. *Top Jobs in Whitehall: Appointments and Promotions in the Senior Civil Service*, Report of an RIPA Working Group, Royal Institute of Public Administration, 1987.
2. David Howells, 'Marks & Spencer and the Civil Service: a Comparison of Culture and Methods', *Public Administration* 59, 3, Autumn 1981.
3. Sir Robert Armstrong, *The Duties and Responsibilities of Civil Servants in Relation to Ministers*, Cabinet Office, 25 February 1985.
4. Armstrong, op. cit., and *Parl. Deb.*, Commons, 2 December 1987, cols 572–5.
5. House of Commons, Treasury and Civil Service Committee, Sub-Committee, Session 1985–86, *Civil Servants and Ministers:* Duties and Responsibilities, Minutes of Evidence, Wednesday, 26 February 1986, a 857.
6. House of Commons, Seventh Report from the Treasury and Civil Service Committee, Session 1985–86, HC 92, para. 4.16.
7. Cmnd 9841 'Civil Servants and Members: Government Response to the Seventh Report from the Treasury and Civil Service Committee, Session 1985–86, HC 92', HMSO, London, 1986.
8. Parl. Deb., Commons, 2 December 1987, col. 575.
9. Albert O. Hirschman, *Exit, Voice and Loyalty: Responses to Decline in Organisations, Firms and States*, Harvard University Press, 1972.
10. Martin Wiener, *English Culture and the Decline of the Industrial Spirit*, 1850–1980, Cambridge University Press, 1982.
11. Corelli Barnett, *The Audit of War*, Macmillan, London, 1986.
12. Michael Elliott, 'Ministers and Officials: towards new constitutional arrangements', paper presented to RIPA Conference, September 1984.
13. Oral intervention at 'Scarman seminar', London, January 1988.
14. Quoted in Cabinet Office (MPO), Heads of Division Notice, 'Prime Minister's Statement', 26 February 1985.
15. Parl. Deb., Commons, loc. cit.
16. Quoted in William Plowden, 'What Prospects for the Civil Service?', *Public Administration*, 63, 4, Winter 1985.
17. Patrick McAuslan, 'The Royal Prerogative as a Threat to the Rule of Law', *Independent*, 27 January 1988.
18. Efficiency Unit, Report to the Prime Minister, *Improving Management in Government: the Next Steps*, HMSO, London, 1988.

12 Conclusion: The Party's Over

Michael Elliott

As Richard Holme sketched out in his introduction to these essays, the overweening emphasis in British modern constitutional history on the sovereignty of parliament has had an unintended corollary. Parliamentary government has become party government, and party government, because of the salient features of the British electoral system, has become two-party – more accurately, alternating-party – government.

It would be foolish to deny the merits of such a system. It can be argued that the obligation of the party not in power to oppose that which is, coupled with the protection, and facilities, given to this act of opposition, are a rough and ready British equivalent of more formal systems of rights and entitlements for individuals. Britain is not, in the grand sweep of things, a notably undemocratic, unfree, society. If party government has helped preserve such British freedoms and democratic practices, good for party government.

Yet quite apart from questions as to whether party government suceeds in its own terms, it has one indisputably doleful effect on political debate. It forces protagonists to be with someone, or against them. It sets peoples apart from each other; it presupposes a dialectic without allowing the possibility of synthesis. It militates against compromise. That makes sense only if the most crass of two-class analyses of British society is correct.

There is an irony here, for it follows that all those who defend our present constitutional arrangements – Conservatives and judges as much as any Labour theoretician – are duty-bound to ignore the shifting boundaries of class in modern Britain. They are forced to deny that there are cleavages in the polity that depend on national or regional loyalty, or that people may have strong feelings about things that have no resonance in inter-party conflict. Party government aspires to an inclusiveness it can never actually attain. It is not trivial to say that most people are not politicians, not particularly enamoured of those who are, and unlikely to cast their minds in terms predefined for them by a political party. If a man believes in unilateral nuclear disarmament and a free-market economy, who shall speak for him? Who stands for those who are in favour of both European unity and a high-taxation welfare state?

Many of the essays in this collection have, as a subtext, the theme that it is possible to carve out intelligible positions that are somewhere between those usually broadcast and most fervently defended. William Plowden has destroyed the idea that there are only two ways in which the civil service can be viewed; Nicholas Deakin has shown how the localist/centralist debate obscures more than it illuminates; Bernard Crick has (with passion, yet) made the case for devolution, the very essence (in much contemporary debate) of a contemptible half-way house. To dismiss these with a sneer as 'moderate', 'well-meaning', 'utopian', is not good enough; all that does is deny the possibility of any change in constitutional arrangements. To murmur 'impractical' (along with 'unhelpful', the last refuge of the British establishment in a fix) is plain wrong. James Cornford has shown how a freedom of information act can work; Lord Scarman how a bill of rights would operate; Vernon Bogdanor how European institutions can be rendered susceptible to democratic control.

These proposals are not important just because, in their own right, they are intelligible and practical. They are important because our present arrangements plainly do not work. John Grigg's essay is just the latest occasion on which Parliament's bluff has been called, yet it is vital that it is called again and again. The obsession of the national media with what goes on in Parliament (television in the chamber will just make things worse); the lionisation of the great 'House of Commons man'; the sheer thrill of a grand set-piece debate; the excitement of the Prime Minister's performance at Question Time – all this masks an uncomfortable truth.

Consider how we might describe party government to a visiting Martian. Here, we might say, is the Prime Minister, and there, her Cabinet. These men and women are wedded together in party (with duties and obligations as onerous as in any marriage); they sink or swim together, we would say. And if our Martian asked why this 'government' was made up of those we have indicated, we would tell him that they were the leaders of the largest party in the Parliament, whose members were pledged to support those leaders on pain of losing the chance of preferment. The other members of Parliament? They 'oppose', we would reply (here things get tricky). And are they always in a minority? Why, on important things, of course. And if not already perplexed, our Martian might then ask what was the cornerstone of this system. 'The sovereignty of Parliament', we would declaim chests puffed-out; 'Parliament checks and controls the government; its actions have a legal omnicompetence (not granted – you are still with us? – to those of the "government").' This – Bentham cannot be bettered – is nonsense on stilts.

When the 'influence' of Parliament; its restraining role; its tidying-up role; its ability to make or break a political career; its occasional discovery of a decisive voice, independent of government, on important matters, and all the other excuses have been stripped away, what is left? For four or five years, it provides a standing body of support for the government, until the performance of that government is assessed by the electorate. That – usually – is all. Parliamentarians resent the phrase 'lobby-fodder', and do so with a reason; most of the time, that is what they are. (Our Martian friend might remind us that Opposition members are usually not even that important.)

Into this increasingly rotten basket Britain has lobbed all its constitutional eggs. Limited territorial autonomy, of the ancient nations or of the local authorities, has been squandered. Individual rights against the state have never been tried. Efforts (the select committees, the ombudsman) to cast light on the processes by which the government exercise power over the rest of us have been feeble when not emasculated. Genuine parliamentary reform, which would have to take the form of a deliberate reduction of the power of party – and electoral reform might well achieve that – so terrifies the establishment that it is hardly polite to mention it in politic company. A separation of powers is dismissed as too American; a constitutional council as too French. Can things go on like this? They can, they can. But they should not; it is time for something new.